THE MURDER OF JOHN SHAKESPEARE

A CENTRALIA COLD CASE

Cary O'Dell and Richard L. Sprehe

Published by The History Press
An imprint of Arcadia Publishing
Charleston, SC
www.historypress.com

First published 2025

Manufactured in the United States

ISBN 9781467170192
Hardcover ISBN 9781540299765

Library of Congress Control Number: 2025944793

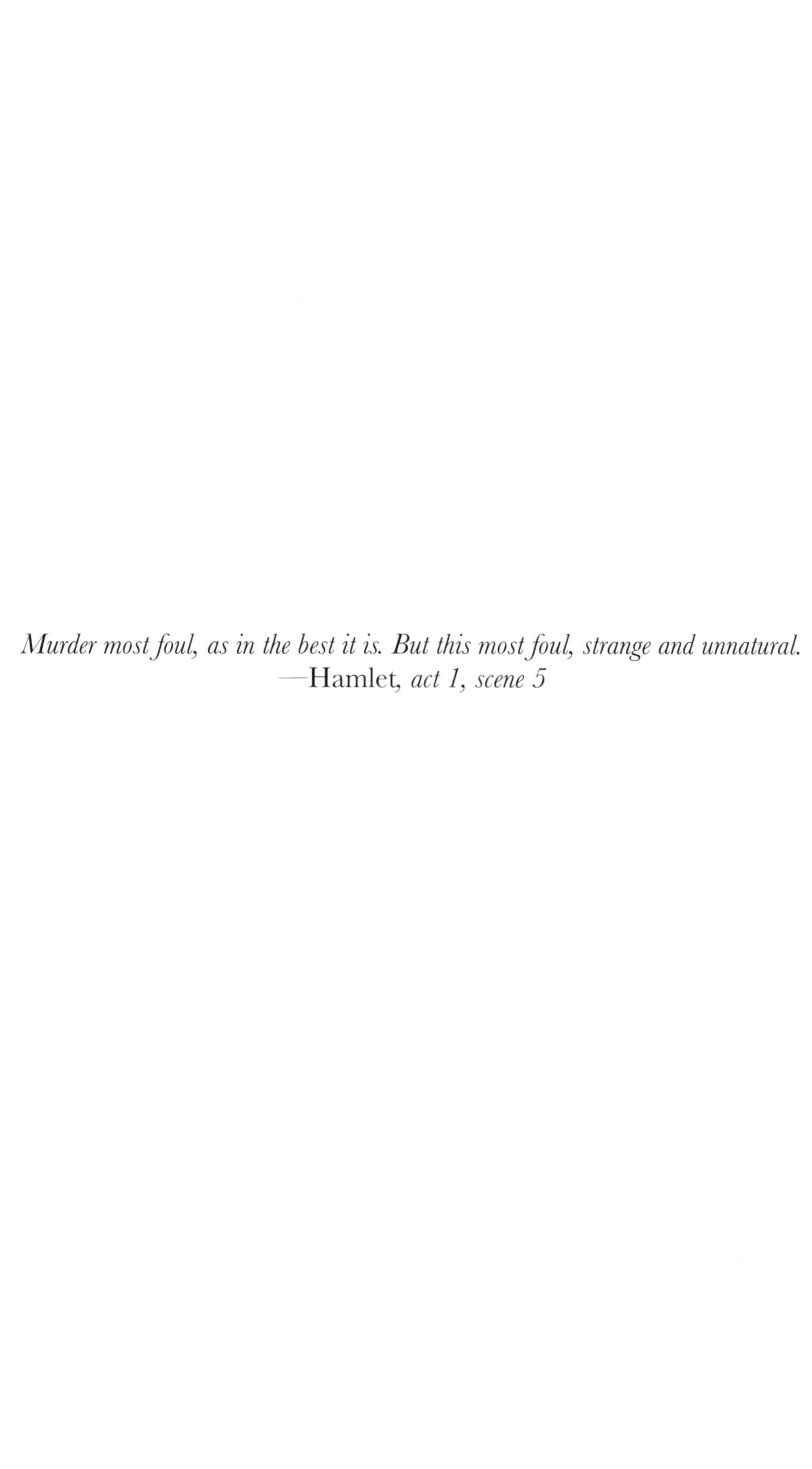

Murder most foul, as in the best it is. But this most foul, strange and unnatural.
—Hamlet, *act 1, scene 5*

CONTENTS

ACKNOWLEDGEMENTS

This book simply could not have been written without my coauthor, Richard Sprehe. He is a researcher without peer. And his doggedness and resourcefulness are outdistanced only by his generosity.

Thank you to Rob Barton, who first suggested that I "take a look" at the Shakespeare case.

Thank you too to Ashley Casseday and Stephen Garland, whose entertaining and highly informative *Keep It Weird*: "Murder in the Midwest" podcast on the crime laid the groundwork for my own inquiry.

Thank you to all the individuals who so candidly spoke to me about this difficult topic, especially the members of the Shakespeare family.

Thank you to Tom Denton, Theresa Greenwood, and Dolores Ford Mobley.

Appreciation to G.H. Beckmeyer for his diligent proofreading contributions.

Special thanks to the Centralia Police Department and the City of Centralia, Illinois.

I'd also like to thank the following, whose great interest in this subject was always appreciated and always served to propel me forward: Julie

Goforth, Meghan Holly, Christian Balistreri, Deb Earhart, Tonya Moran, and Stacie Seifrit-Griffin.

As always, thank you to Karmon Runquist and Mike Heintz.

Richard Sprehe would like to acknowledge Cary O'Dell for his time, dedication and skill, which made this book possible.

And from both of us, of course, thank you to John W. Shakespeare. Despite the lack of closure regarding his life, may he have nevertheless found an everlasting peace.

INTRODUCTION

This book does not solve the mystery of who killed John Shakespeare.

Unfortunately, after all this time—a full half a century—this crime will probably never be solved and will simply join the wide pantheon of long, enduring mysteries.

Additionally, even if this case were officially "solved" tomorrow and a name or names of the guilty were made public, there would remain those who would question it. After all, technically, we have solved the Kennedy assassination and the Lindbergh kidnapping and other similar crimes, but that has not stopped an untold number of books, articles and blog posts from continually being published and purporting to tell the "true story" of these famous or infamous events.

A pre-hippie John Shakespeare, circa 1965. *Authors' collection.*

What this book does do is gather the key facts about the Shakespeare case and present them in a way that is accurate and as truthful as possible based on the accounts and records that we have available to us fifty years after the crime took place.

In that process, it is our hope that this book will also clear up some of the unfounded rumors and half-truths that have tenaciously shadowed this case (and this town and the reputation of the late Mr. Shakespeare and many others) for the past fifty years.

Shakespeare's monogram, in metal, in the ironwork at the side door of his Centralia home. *Authors' collection.*

In no way is this book meant to accuse or smear any persons alive or dead. This is a work of reportage. Every statement, every sentence, every quote in this book is drawn from official police reports, newspaper articles, or original interviews. And ultimately, we have no way of verifying the veracity of any of those sources, so we can only take them at face value.

Further, any speculation within these pages is strictly the conclusion of the authors, neither of whom is a professional investigator or law enforcement official. Nothing is intended to malign anyone but, instead, to create a discussion and, from that, hopefully generate a thorough, better understanding of this crime and therefore bring us closer to its truth.

1
THE VICTIM

Despite the obviously central role that he plays in the crime (and this book), it is important to remember that John W. Shakespeare was more than his murder.

Shakespeare (or "Shake" as he was often called) was a man of great intellect, curiosity, generosity, and ingenuity and one who was also inventive and funny. He was a man of great passions, with a certain playfulness, and as one person who knew him said, he was "an inspiration."[1]

John William Shakespeare was born on September 18, 1905, in Kalamazoo, Michigan.[2] He was one of four children born to the coyly named William Shakespeare Jr.[3] (Years later, when John would inevitably be asked if he was related to *the* William Shakespeare, he'd reply, "Yes, he's my father," a line that was, in fact, true.)[4]

John's father—this *other* William Shakespeare—was born in 1869.[5] From early on, he had great business acumen. In 1889, with a man named Garrett Low, he co-owned the Kalamazoo Shutter Company, a manufacturer of camera shutters.[6]

From his youth, William was an avid fisherman. And demonstrating a mechanical bent that he would genetically bequeath to at least one of his children, in 1896, he developed a type of level-winding fishing reel that helped revolutionize the fishing industry.[7] Later, he went on to develop other major fishing innovations, including fiberglass fishing rods and a monofilament fishing line.[8]

In 1905, Shakespeare formed his own company to manufacture and sell the reel and other fishing innovations.[9] The company eventually adopted the name the William Shakespeare Jr. Company (later changed to the Shakespeare Company). By 1902, the company had over a dozen employees and was selling its merchandise nationwide. In 1908, the Shakespeare Company launched its enduring slogan, "Built Like a Watch."[10] Later still, the company expanded into a variety of other non-fishing products, including boat oars, dog leads and hunting clothes. It also published booklets on good fishing techniques. In 1970, the company relocated from Michigan to Columbia, South Carolina, where it is still headquartered today.[11]

John Shakespeare's mother was Lhea Chase West Shakespeare, William Shakespeare's second wife. Lhea gave her husband two sons, John in 1905 and Henry in 1909. (John also had two older half siblings, Mildred and Monroe, from William Shakespeare's first marriage to Cora Monroe Shakespeare.)[12]

According to one source, the young John Shakespeare enjoyed a "golden spoon" upbringing.[13] And certainly, thanks to his father's company, he did grow up with a privilege that many young people at that time did not enjoy. Yet young John was expected to work. And he did work, for a time, in the family business.[14]

After graduating from high school, John Shakespeare attended the city's Kalamazoo College. In 1924, his college newspaper, the *Kalamazoo College Index*, announced Shakespeare's recent winning of a photo snapshot contest.[15] In 1928, Shakespeare served as vice president of the school's Chemistry Club.[16]

Later, Shakespeare headed off to study mathematics and physics at the Carnegie Institute of Technology before continuing his graduate studies at Harvard.[17]

Following graduation, Shakespeare returned briefly to the family business,[18] but fishing was not among his myriad interests. Further, younger brother Henry seemed to have assumed the role as his family's heir apparent, and Shake felt he'd always be in second place. It seems John always wanted to be his own man.[19] John eventually left the company. Later, in a typical self-deprecating style, when asked why he departed the family firm, Shake said, "Every department I'd be put into, I'd just wreck."[20]

Shakespeare joined the navy in 1940. In the service, Shake eventually rose to the rank of commander. He specialized in naval matters of intelligence and photography. Later, during World War II, most of his time was spent in the Pacific theater.[21]

After his service, John pursued his interests in, among other areas, the oil business. By 1950, he was living in Evansville, Indiana, and working for the

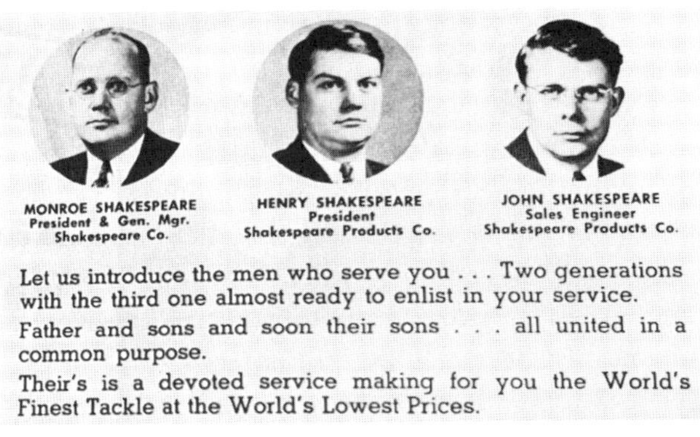

A young John Shakespeare, circa 1941, in a catalogue for the family fish-and-tackle business. *Authors' collection.*

McCummings Drilling Company.[22] Around this time, Shakespeare also began to enter other enterprises, including pursuing a budding interest in automobiles, especially sports cars and foreign-made vehicles. He would go on to own and operate car dealerships in Indiana, Illinois and Florida.[23] (The latter supposedly contained an "elaborate showroom.")[24]

John Shakespeare moved to southern Illinois in 1950.[25] Interestingly, at the time, newspapers in both Illinois and Indiana made note of his relocation. He moved to become part of a freshly formed oil company. Earlier that year, a friend of his, Harry C. Temple, approached him about starting an energy company alongside a third partner, Jim McCarty, a petroleum engineer. In their outreach to Shakespeare, they asked him for two things: starting capital and to use his name for their fledgling business. Shakespeare agreed to both.[26]

The Shakespeare Oil Company, incorporated in 1950, is still in business today. Its building sits on Main Street in the town of Salem, Illinois.[27]

Despite the new company being headquartered in Salem (with its 1950 population of around six thousand), Shakespeare apparently opted instead to live a few miles away in the "big city" of Centralia (its 1950 population was around thirteen thousand). In Centralia, Shakespeare moved into a handsome brick home located at 514 South Pine Street, which, at the time, was probably considered to be in one of the city's "better" neighborhoods. Though Shakespeare would also later maintain residences in Florida (Singer Island) and Switzerland,[28] this 1,589-square-foot home was his primary residence for the rest of his life.[29] The two-bedroom and one-bath home sat on .44 of an acre, and though he never owned it, Shakespeare made a variety of upgrades and changes to it.[30] Along with the wrought-iron initials by the home's side entrance, he installed a recessed light exactly above where he kept his favorite chair in his living room, all the better to read.[31] In addition, in the basement of the home, down its small flight of stairs with its small landing and turn halfway down, he added linoleum to one section of the partitioned space; that became his office. The rest of the basement was also developed enough to make it an efficient, workable environment for tinkering with engines. Several long fluorescent lights ran along one wall, equally spaced apart, creating room for four different motors if John was so inclined.[32]

Not long after moving in, Shakespeare built a large detached garage directly behind the house. But this was not an ordinary garage. Shakespeare had a quarry-tiled heated floor built in so that he could be comfortable and

Left: Shakespeare Oil, located in Salem, Illinois, as it looks today. *Authors' collection.*

Below: The Shakespeare house at 514 South Pine in Centralia as it looks today. *Authors' collection.*

Opposite: The interior and exterior of the garage behind the South Pine house as it looks today. *Authors' collection.*

warm while working under a vehicle.[33] Also in one segment of the garage was a hydraulic lift so that he didn't have to crawl under at all.[34] Both structures are still standing today.

Over the years, Shakespeare followed a variety of passions and hobbies, and luckily for him, he possessed the freedom and money to pursue them fully.

For a time, he considered himself a gourmet cook, whipping up sun-cooked strawberry jam or exotic, complicated pâtés. Then, for a time, he dabbled in horticulture, raising orchids. For his floral interest, he even built a greenhouse onto the side of his home. How good he was at these various endeavors is open to debate, but Shakespeare certainly seemed to enjoy himself.[35]

Throughout all these pastimes, Shakespeare's love of being physically active remained. He jogged, swam, skied (snow and water), and even skydived.[36] (In fact, he skydived for the first time *after* he turned sixty years old.)[37] Later, in Centralia, he had the first home gym set up that anyone in town could remember.[38]

Shakespeare was also a great tinkerer. Rumor has it that he once even built his own color TV.[39] Later, for one of his cars, he created a device that sat on the dash and calculated the car's gas mileage, long before fuel efficiency became a common American concern.[40] Later, Shakespeare gained a kind of local fame for owning the very first microwave oven that anyone had ever seen or even heard of.[41] And then, sprouting up from various towers around his house, he erected multiple antennas, as Shake liked radios, hi-fi stereo systems, and electronics of all kinds.[42] (All these antennas would later lead to a rather far-fetched rumor that Shakespeare, who did work in intelligence when he was in the navy, was actually working for the government still, only this time as a spy!)

Testifying to Shakespeare's many diverse interests are the wide assortment of licenses and ID cards that were found among his possessions after his death: he was a member of the Aspen Ski Club; he was certified by the American Red Cross in water safety; he was a "member" of the Associated American Artists, an art gallery in New York City; he had an Indiana hunting and fishing license; he was an "Official Photographer" for the U.S. Navy; and he still held on to his "chauffeur's" license, another holdover from his days in the military.[43]

But John Shakespeare's greatest passion was for cars.

In the early 1950s, Shakespeare began to position himself as one of the nation's foremost automobile collectors. In September 1956, he made national news when he acquired, as the newspapers put it, "one of the biggest, rarest and most costly autos ever built."[44] This car was a 1933 Bugatti La Royale with "limousine coachwork." It measured twenty feet long, seven feet wide and six and a half feet high. It weighed three tons.[45] Only seven of these mammoth machines were ever built before the Great Depression destroyed the market for such hyper-luxurious transportation.[46] So, in 1956, the fact that this monster of a vehicle was coming to reside in southern Illinois was big news, and newspapers all over printed articles about its acquisition with Shake photographed standing (and being dwarfed) beside it. After the car arrived in Chicago via freighter, Shakespeare picked it up and drove it down to Centralia himself—a distance of about three hundred miles.[47]

Earlier, Shakespeare had purchased a three-hundred-horsepower Ferrari. In 1954, he had fun showing it off at least once at a Belleville car show.[48] He would eventually own four Ferraris and become a friend of company founder Enzo Ferrari.

Over the years, Shake owned a variety of other expensive, exotic vehicles, including a couple of Porsches. But it was Bugattis—those classic, smart, sporty roadsters made in France—that seemed (at least for a time) to be his favorite. His first Bugatti purchase was of a Type 55 built in 1932.[49] This was soon followed by twenty-nine more! By the mid-1950s, Centralia's own John Shakespeare owned the largest collection of Bugattis anywhere in the world. And while some were stored in the large, free-standing garage behind his Centralia home, others were stored in a building Shake rented over in Hoffman, Illinois, a town about six miles west of Centralia.[50]

Along with collecting cars, Shake liked to race them. Shake did his first race in 1953. In 1954, Shakespeare competed, as a co-driver, with Luigi Chinetti, in the Pan American road race being held in Mexico City. The duo eventually finished fifth.[51] Other races Shakespeare participated in took place in Florida and the Caribbean; he even once raced at Le Mans.[52] He also raced in Wisconsin. On Wisconsin's Elkhart Lake speedway, he experienced but survived a wreck.[53] If not racing himself, Shakespeare sometimes sponsored other racers, including the legendary Red Byron.[54]

Shakespeare also liked to tinker with his cars. To the dismay of many who were invited to see his Bugattis, they often saw that the cars had been partially dismantled, with various removed parts scattered all over the floor of the

garage. Such a practice is usually considered a verboten action by car lovers/enthusiasts. Additionally, whether in Hoffman or Centralia, the valuable roadsters often sat uncovered and collecting dust.[55]

But many of his cars were roadworthy, and he even sometimes drove them up to visit family in Michigan.

His nephew Eric recalls "half a dozen" times Uncle John came to visit him and of the vision of his uncle's Ferrari coming up the dirt road to his grandmother's house. He also remembers sitting down at the dinner table and seeing John downing a "big handful of vitamins" to begin his meal. And Eric, who was in his teens in the early 1970s when John visited, also remembers his uncle's tales of traveling on the *QE2* and of going car shopping in Italy. Once, some years prior, John gave Eric a Matchbox car that totally matched the new sportscar he had just bought.[56]

Other family members have other memories. Eric's brother Dan remembers their uncle's interest in gardening and, after one visit where they discussed Dan's nascent vegetable garden, of his uncle sending him a package of green beans seeds that John said were indigenous to Italy. Says Dan today, "He was just this cool guy to us."[57]

Shakespeare's niece Valerie Shakespeare later became a radical visual and conceptual artist. In her 2008 memoir, *It's the Artist Life for Me!*, she recounted once driving with her "favorite uncle" in one of his Bugattis all the way from Kalamazoo to Centralia. She wrote, "He was an erudite and extravagant traveling companion but I soon found out why he was so anxious for me to come along. The Bugatti's windshield wipers were manual! He needed me to operate them when it was raining! Oh! My arms got sore."[58]

After about ten years of ownership, however, Shakespeare received an offer for his Bugatti collection. But first, the potential buyer—Frenchman Fritz Schlumpf—sent a fellow car aficionado to Centralia to inspect the

Opposite: John Shakespeare with some of his prized auto collection. *From the Centralia Sentinel.*

Top: Shakespeare tinkering with one of his cars. *From the Centralia Sentinel.*

Bottom: Some of Shakespeare's prized cars seen in disrepair. *From the Centralia Sentinel.*

collection. The dispatched inspector, Bob Shaw, was not impressed.[59] He wrote back to Schlumpf:

> *The Shakespeare collection is housed in a facility formerly used as a foundry. Most of the cars are in a dirt-floored building. The roof leaks, windows are broken, and birds are nesting inside. The better cars are in a heated, concrete-floored shop. Practically every car is in some state of disassembly; none has run in eighteen months.*[60]

Nevertheless, the size of the collection was far too enticing for the eager and wealthy Frenchman. Still, it took some intense negotiations, spread out over the next fourteen months, before the two men agreed on a final price; Shakespeare finally sold the collection for $85,000.[61]

Even at the time, $85,000 for thirty of these highly collectible cars was considered a bargain basement price, leading later to speculation that Shakespeare was in need of cash and, hence, was ready to accept almost any amount for his hoard. But at the time, Shakespeare stated to the press, "It's awful easy to get into too many hobbies. Right now, I'm more interested in sports."[62]

Later still, John repeated a story to several people that when he demanded $85,000 for the collection, he expected Schlumpf to balk. But Schlumpf didn't. And Shakespeare had too much integrity to raise the price after the fact—or at least, that was the explanation he gave.[63] Whether this was true or a convenient tale for him to save face is still open to debate.

Finally, in February 1964, the sale was complete, and Shakespeare himself oversaw the loading of his thirty cars onto several double-decker Southern Railway train cars for their shipping from Illinois to New Orleans and then onto a ship for their final journey to France.[64]

The disposition of Shakespeare's collection drew both news attention (it became a story in an issue of *Motor Trend* magazine) and, on the day the shipment began, a variety of curious onlookers. Though Shake was careful to cover each steering wheel in plastic and remove each of their iconic hood ornaments, the vehicles had no further protection for their long trip to their new home.[65]

Today, the thirty Bugattis are part of the Musée National de l'Automobile located in Mulhouse, France.[66]

The sale of his Bugattis did not end Shakespeare's love affair with all things on wheels, however. For the rest of his life, he owned a small fleet of expensive cars and had fun tooling around town in them.[67] According to

John preps one of his Bugattis for shipment after they were sold to an overseas buyer. *From the Centralia Sentinel.*

his nephew Eric, sometimes, to amuse himself, Shakespeare would buy old junk vehicles and equip them with hot rod engines. Once his ride was newly configured, he'd pull up alongside local "cool" kids and challenge them to a race. When they'd take him up on this challenge, he'd joyfully leave them in the dust.[68]

Eric told another story of a time when his uncle was in Florida and needed a new car. Shakespeare went to a local Cadillac dealership but didn't dress up too much beforehand. When the salesman saw Shakespeare looking a little disheveled, the salesman just ignored him, passing him off as something of bum. Then John went across the street to the Chrysler dealership and paid cash for a brand-new New Yorker. Shakespeare then drove back across the street and honked his horn so that the salesman who ignored him saw him. And with that, Shakespeare lifted his middle finger and then drove away.[69]

But if cars ever became less of a passion for Shakespeare, they were soon replaced by all things fitness. As mentioned, Shakespeare had one of the first home gyms—fitted out with a system of weights and pullies—that anyone could recall.[70] His commitment to his physique was so pronounced, his home bore a variety of large—actually oversized—mirrors in which Shakespeare could, seemingly, keep visual track of his fitness journey.[71] He was famous—almost infamous—for his frequent jogs around town, usually clad only in a pair of red running shorts. Eschewing sneakers, Shake usually ran barefoot.[72]

John Shakespeare watched his diet too. He did not drink coffee or soda, and in 1966, when Centralia was debating the merits of putting fluoride in their drinking water, Shakespeare appeared at a city council meeting and vehemently testified against incorporating this "poison" into the city's water supply.[73]

All this physical effort must have paid off, as Shake remained in remarkably good shape throughout his life. Though only five feet, five inches tall, he maintained a slim 145-pound frame. In a letter he sent to a friend in the early 1970s, when he was in his sixties, he wrote, "I recently had a physical exam. The Doctor seemed disappointed as he could not find anything much wrong with me."[74]

In his youth, Shake was described as ruggedly handsome and as having the looks of a soap star. But later, in the early 1970s he grew his (gray) hair out and sported a beard and seemed to like his aging hippie vibe. He set off his whole look with a pair of black horn-rimmed glasses.

In 1960, after ten years' involvement with Shakespeare's Oil—though mostly as a "silent partner"[75]—John Shakespeare divested himself from the company, though it retained his name and he continued to own an oil lease up in Illinois' White County.[76] (Sometime in the 1950s, John and his brother Henry also sold off 640 acres of land that they owned near Orlando, Florida. They sold it rather cheaply. Later, that land became part of Walt Disney World, and John described that low-priced transaction as one of the bigger mistakes of his life.)[77]

In March 1955, in Centralia, John was welcomed into the local Rotary Club.[78] Not long after joining, Shakespeare entertained the Rotarians by serving as chairman for a special screening of a film on fishing. The film, which featured professional fisherman Ben Hardesty, was part of a Rotarians luncheon.[79]

In June 1973, after he and some fellow Centralians took a trip to Australia and New Zealand,[80] Shake presented a slideshow about their exotic trip to the local Lions Club.[81]

Though a transplant to town, Shakespeare proved to be quite civically minded over the years. He was always happy to loan some of his exotic cars to the city for use in local parades, and in October 1955, he donated one of his Volkswagens to the Centralia police force. Equipped later with a flashing red light on top, a siren, and loudspeaker, this "bug" was to be used by the city for traffic safety.[82] (For tooling around town, however, Shake usually used his Chevy Suburban.)[83]

However, being "community-minded" did not mean he was always in agreement with Centralia's city bosses. Besides the fluoride issue, once, when he decided that the city was charging too much for water, Shakespeare decided to dig his own well. This included dynamite and blasting a hole on his property to create it.[84]

Not far from where he blasted the well, he erected a windmill.[85]

Above: Remnant of the backyard well that John Shakespeare dug for himself. *Authors' collection.*

Right: A second backyard folly: remnant of a windmill Shakespeare constructed. *Authors' collection.*

Throughout his time in Centralia, Shakespeare was also involved with the local troop of Explorer Scouts. For well over a decade, Shakespeare was known to underwrite and serve as chaperone for various camping, canoeing, and rafting trips that the boys took to places like Minnesota, Missouri, and even Canada.[86]

When he was a boy, Tim Loughran was in the Explorer troop during the time Shake was a troop leader. Loughran remembers taking at least three camping/canoeing trips with Shake and the other Scouts. He remembers Shakespeare as an exemplary Scout leader, a "role model." He says today, "We loved the guy."[87]

Fellow former Explorer Steve Duensing concurs and vividly recalls not only Shake on the trips but also his early health advocacy. Once, around the evening campfire, while the others waited for the canned corn to cook over the flame, Shake drank down the corn juice from the can, telling the boys that that was the healthiest part.[88]

Craig Hensley was also on a couple of those trips. He was not only an Explorer in Shake's troop (for "five or six years")[89] but also lived near him. In addition to the trips, which included eight to ten others and fellow local leader Ron Goff, Hensley remembers a ride that Shake once gave him in his Ferrari. He also remembers when Shake turned his large backyard garage into an inside basketball court in winter.[90]

Kirby Dipert was an Explorer around 1967 and went along with Shake and fellow Scout leader Ron Goff and all the other Scouts on a couple of the group's canoe and hiking trips. Dipert also sometimes hung with the group at Shake's Pine Street home, where Shake would demonstrate the latest gadget he was working on or show off one of his exotic cars or allow the kids to jump on the trampoline he owned behind his Pine Street home.[91]

Mark Stedelin, who was one of four Stedelin brothers in the troop at one time, once drove up to Canada with Shake and some of the other boys and ended up sharing a tent with him for much of their trip. Stedelin calls Shake "an inspiration" who always gave "sage" advice on everything from how to ride a motorcycle to the benefits of the emerging field of isometric exercise. Stedelin says Shake was "a good guy and a good leader."[92]

Only a few months before his death, Shakespeare was honored by the local Scouts with a dinner to thank him for his service to the organization. At that time, Shakespeare was quoted as saying that he thought he enjoyed the activities as much as the boys did.[93]

Shakespeare always seemed to be on the go. Along with spending some of the year at his other residences in Florida and Switzerland, he traveled extensively—to the Bahamas or to Asia. He brought back wonderful artifacts that ended up in his Centralia home mixed in with the expensive paintings he also collected.[94] He went on ski trips too—to Utah, Colorado, and other locales. In early 1974, he took a ski trip with some friends, the McCallum family of Independence, Missouri. Found among Shakespeare's personal effects, a lovely handwritten letter from Mrs. McCallum to John, dated February 13, 1974, along with some group pictures taken on the slopes evidence a warm and wonderful holiday. (Mrs. McCallum concluded her letter with a playful postscript: "Did my daughter really have the audacity to give your goatee a tug?")[95]

When Shakespeare was in town, he often hung out at the local grocery store owned by his friends Raymond and Rose Smith. Then, other times, joined by friends like Lee Hanon or Harold F. Petrea, he headed down to Okawville, Illinois, to the mineral springs spa that was located there.[96] In fact, Shakespeare had an appointment for a massage at the springs later in the week that he was killed.[97]

Considering all this, it's odd that so many articles published after his death call him a "recluse."[98]

Shakespeare had an active mind, too. Along with all his at-home tinkering, Shakespeare, in the early 1970s, began to explore developments in cell therapy, as he felt that they might help extend his life.[99] Around this time, he was also nursing an interest in non-Keynesian economic systems.

He was enrolled in language classes, which he took once or twice a week, over in Belleville, Illinois.[100] Shakespeare could pay for all of this not only thanks to his family's wealth but also due to his wise and active investing over the years. In his investing, he was a risk-taker. Via Albert F. Gibson, his Massachusetts-based financial consultant (though the two would later have a major falling out in early 1975),[101] Shake invested aggressively in silver; in various oil companies; and in Tormex, Rosario Resources, Northgate, and H.F. Systems.[102]

Shake also had a decided interest in—and put considerable cash into—what was called the Monte Sole project, a Swiss-based offshoot of the Progress Foundation. PF (as it was known) was the creation of American economist Edward C. Harwood, whom Shakespeare had met in the 1930s.[103] Like Shakespeare, Harwood was a believer in the gold standard, and Shakespeare had, apparently, at one time benefited from Harwood's investing advice. By the 1970s, Shake was investing heavily in this would-be utopian community that Harwood was trying to build in the Swiss countryside.[104] It was something that, in a letter from January

1974, his money advisor, Gibson, strongly advised him against, seemingly, to no avail.[105]

Unfortunately, Harwood wasn't the only rather dubious individual Shakespeare seemed to have had faith in. Among some of his correspondence is a 1973 letter directing Gibson to send $50,000 to a man named Michael Oliver located in Carson City, Nevada.[106] Oliver, among other questionable ventures, attempted in the early 1970s to establish his own micronation on one of the islands of the Minerva Reefs. But the king of nearby Tonga, who claimed ownership of the land, thought otherwise. After Oliver and company occupied the land for about three weeks, Tonga-led troops reclaimed the island.[107]

Rumors abounded that Shakespeare was prepping for doomsday at this time as well. Shake thought that putting his wealth into gold rather than the more nebulous cash currency was a better plan. He did mention his fear of being known as living in a house with ample amounts of stored gold.[108]

By May 1975, John Shakespeare's life was proceeding apace. He was supposedly planning a trip to Dallas in July to meet with the famous physician Dr. Kenneth H. Cooper.[109] Cooper would later become one of the first in the medical community to espouse the benefits of aerobic exercise.[110] Shakespeare was open to medical science's newest methods and theories of extending human life.[111] And he was only a few days away from going on his latest trip with the Explorers—this time to Missouri for several days.[112] After that, he was planning to take an extended leave from Centralia to live in Switzerland (for perhaps as long as eighteenth months). For his life living abroad, Shakespeare had already secured an apartment (a condo, part of the Monte Sole project) overseas and had already been making arrangements to have both a car—a specially ordered BMW—and a motorcycle delivered there to be at his disposal.[113]

But he would not live to make either trip.

2
THE CRIME

John Shakespeare's body was found in the early evening of May 8, 1975.[1] Police records differ slightly as to the exact time he was found, listing both 8:02 p.m.[2] and 8:12 p.m.[3]

Ken Buchanan, at CPD headquarters, took the initial call and dispatched Officer Stanley Pokojski to the scene. Pokojski soon notified his headquarters to contact and dispatch both the coroner and the crime lab tech. In short order, police shift commander Lieutenant Gene Qualls and Officer Paul Ritter also arrived at the Pine Street home. They were soon followed by Officers Richard Forehand and Jim Glasgow and then Michael C. Geurin at 8:30 p.m. Crime technician Willam Austin arrived at the scene at approximately 9:45 p.m.[4]

The body had been discovered by Shakespeare's longtime (twenty-plus years) property caretaker/handyman Ralph Porter. According to Porter, he had gone into the house that evening, gaining entry with his own key, to get some light bulbs. That's when he saw Shakespeare.[5]

Immediately, Porter ran to the garage behind the house, which had its own telephone, and called the police.[6]

Shakespeare's body was found in the basement of his home. The basement was only a semifinished one; it contained a handful of smaller rooms, one of which Shakespeare used as an office.[7] Shakespeare may have already been in the basement when he was attacked. He was found lying on his right side on the concrete of the basement's boiler room, a small room in the northeast corner of the basement.[8] Pooled around his

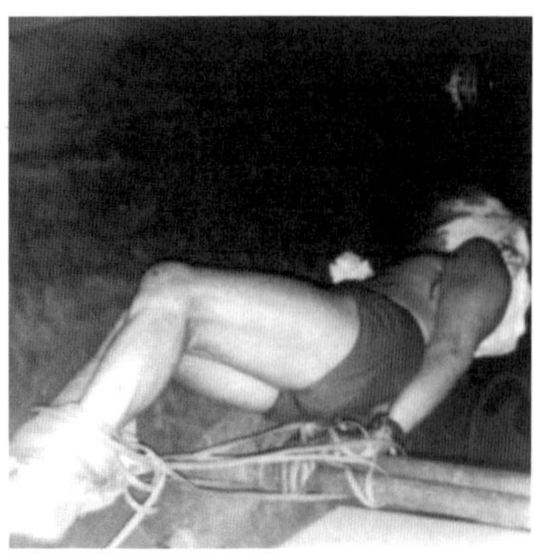

The body of John Shakespeare as it was discovered in the basement of his home. Note the towels tied around his head, his wristwatch still on his wrist and the tied restraints. *Centralia Police Department.*

head was a thick lagoon of congealed blood.[9]

Interestingly, that subterranean section of the house, encased by eight-inch concrete walls and further insulated by the presence of the greenhouse above it, might have been the most soundproof place in the Pine Street structure. Was this location picked by chance, or was it chosen by his killer(s) to keep the sound of him or of their gun undetected? If the latter, did the killer or killers already know the layout of Shakespeare's home?

At the time of his death, Shakespeare was clad only in his trademark red running shorts. Though one couldn't tell immediately, he was killed by a single gunshot to the head. His feet were bound with a piece of fabric, later described as either yellow or tan in color and possibly torn from a shirt, and his hands cuffed—in a pair of police-grade handcuffs—behind his back. A yellow electrical cord had been used (repeatedly knotted, in square, or "reef," knots, which according to police would be best known by "Boy scouts, sailors, etc.") to tie him to a pipe in the basement. His face was covered with two bright beach towels. A blood-stained blue bandana, later speculated to be a gag once stuffed in his mouth, was found tied around his neck; he must have been able to get loose from it. Another blue rag was found on the floor just outside of the boiler room.[10]

Later, one of the local police officers described the crime as the work of a "sadist."[11] Stanley Pokojski, the first officer on the scene, later stated that, to him, "Shakespeare obviously knew the person [who] murdered him."[12] As Jim Glasgow took photos of the crime scene in the basement, police went upstairs to look for clues and whatever might have been taken. But the home—though far from tidy—did not give the appearance of having been ransacked.[13] While a few drawers were open, and Shakespeare's sock drawer was said to be especially disrupted, nothing had been dumped out. Similarly, no area seemed to suggest that any sort of struggle had taken place.[14]

Later, with the aid of Ralph Porter, the police found only three items to be missing from the home: a jade necklace that had supposedly belonged to Shakespeare's mother (though other pieces of her jewelry remained untouched); a can of mace (Shakespeare was known to have had two at one time, one stored in the bedroom and one in the living room, but one was now missing); and a radio, a police-type scanner used to overhear local emergency transmissions.[15] Also believed to be taken though never completely verified was a briefcase that Shakespeare kept by his bed that might have held a large quantity of foreign currency.[16] Since the currency would have little value in the United States, was the attaché taken just to be used to remove the other items from the house?

The paltriness of what was taken—and the removed items themselves—confused investigators. Shakespeare's home contained all sorts of electronics, camera equipment, Asian antiques and other valuable items, but they had been left untouched. Even the expensive watch that Shakespeare had on his person when he was killed was left behind and is now part of the collection of evidence at the Centralia Police Department.

Though Shakespeare's wallet was empty of any cash that might have once been in it, there were those who said Shake never carried much cash with him anyway, preferring instead the ease of the new world of credit cards.[17] Shake had several of those in his wallet; they were untouched.

Also *not* found at the crime scene were any latent fingerprints. The night Shakespeare was found, detectives dusted much of the crime scene and came up empty-handed.[18]

As strange as what was missing was what was found in the home: a sixteen-ounce Pepsi bottle, half empty, was sitting on the kitchen counter.[19] Shakespeare, the health advocate that he was, never drank soft drinks. So how did that get there, and who left it behind?

Then, perhaps even odder is, in February 1977, a letter from the offices of the Illinois Bureau of Investigation was sent to Centralia official Kermit Justice, and it lists three previously unmentioned pieces of evidence that were found at or quite near the scene of the Shakespeare murder.[20] They were:

one paperback book
one Marvel comic book
one piece of blue paper

Further information about any of them is not listed, though it does say that they had been checked by the IBI for fingerprints—with no results.[21]

By the time police and medical crews departed the basement that night, a crowd of onlookers had gathered outside of Shakespeare's home. They were attracted by the lights of the police cars and ambulance. Alerted by her friend Shubert Fox (who was also a friend of Shakespeare's), Judith Joy, a local reporter for the *Centralia Sentinel*, rushed to the scene.[22]

The murder of John Shakespeare would be the paper's front-page story the next day.

3
THE AUTOPSY

John Shakespeare was pronounced dead at the scene—his home's basement—at 8:10 p.m. on May 8, 1975.[1]

After Shakespeare's body was discovered and crime scene photos were taken (by Officers Jim Glasgow and Richard Forehand),[2] the corpse, fully covered with a sheet, was loaded onto a gurney and then removed from the basement of the home via the home's side entrance before being placed into the back of an ambulance parked outside of Shakespeare's Pine Street residence.[3]

One of the first people allowed into that basement was Roger Campbell, the deputy coroner for Marion County and the founder of his own ambulance service in Centralia.[4] His company began in 1973 and continues today. When interviewed recently, Campbell's recollections of that night differ from many other accounts. "I don't remember any handcuffs being taken off of Shakespeare," he said. He also didn't notice any broken glass—a detail that was to become an important part of this murder investigation. Campbell also took notice of the apparent lack of struggle evident on Shakespeare's body: there were no pronounced scratches or marks.[5]

After Shakespeare's body left Pine Street (where a considerable crowd of onlookers had gathered during the evening), it was transported to Centralia's St. Mary's Hospital.[6] The next day, the body underwent an autopsy conducted by Dr. Cesar Gallego, a pathologist.[7] (E.E. Perry was actually Marion County's coroner—and the local eye doctor—but he happened to be out of town that evening.)[8]

Police investigators in the basement of Shakespeare's home on the night the body was discovered. *From left to right*: Bill Austin, crime tech; state police officer Mike Guern; and Centralia Police Chief Simon Franklin. *Centralia Police Department.*

One of the first things that Dr. Gallego recorded in his report later that night was that the victim had been dead since "either later afternoon or early evening on the date the body was found."[9]

Both men were later joined at the hospital by a second photographer to take evidentiary photos.[10] A cause of death was easy to determine. In Gallego's report, it is listed simply as "gun shot wound to the head."[11]

Later, all ten of Shakespeare's fingerprints were taken, along with a hair sample and a vial of his blood.[12] (The blood, type O, and the hair samples remain in the evidence boxes at the Centralia PD today.) Also retained as evidence were the two towels that had been wrapped around Shakespeare's head (these, too, are at CPD HQ).[13]

Finally taken from the body was the spent slug of the bullet that killed John Shakespeare. It would later be described as "partially flattened." The bullet—and only that one bullet—had entered the left temple of the victim, traveling upward and into the brain.[14]

A few days later, on May 14, a toxicology report of Shakespeare's blood came back from a Chicago-area lab. Among the results, the blood analysis showed no evidence of ethanol, and it showed zero presence of barbiturates, stimulants or tranquilizers.[15]

In a separate report labeled "Verdict of Coroner's Jury," also filled out that first night, is some biographical information about John Shakespeare. It includes Shakespeare's age (sixty-nine), his home address and a marital status of "Never Married" and lists his occupation as "Oil Company Owner."[16]

Another report conducted after death and after examining the body did make mention of "areas of abrasion…on the right wrist as well as marks of handcuffs. Both ankles also exhibited areas of abrasion probably resulting from [the] binding of the feet."[17]

Then the "Supplementary Report" states that the handcuffs put on Shakespeare were "extremely tight" and "cut into the wrist."[18] In that same report, there is also a notation of "fingernail abrasion" on the "inner aspect of the left arm"; the largest measured 1.5 centimeters in diameter and 6 centimeters long.[19]

In an interview the police later did with Dr. Gallego, he also made note of various "scraps [*sic*]" on both the victim's knees and the arms.[20]

Also on May 14, 1975, Centralia lead detective Simon Franklin was joined by Illinois Bureau of Investigation (IBI) special agent James McCoy and an IBI special agent with the last name Ergon. They went to St. Mary's to personally interview Dr. Gallego.[21] First, Dr. Gallego was asked about his knowledge of S&M and bondage-oriented sex practices. Gallego expressed that he was somewhat familiar with them but noted that, in his examination, he found no evidence of sexual molestation of the victim and no "undue" torture or any other evidence that "would indicate any kind of sexual crime." He also said that he "could see no semen stains" on either Shakespeare's body or clothing.[22]

But, Dr. Gallego added, he "could not examine the rectum area for penetration or semen because of the fact that…[Mr. Shakespeare excreted an] awful lot of stool."[23]

In regard to the small markings on Shakespeare's arms, Dr. Gallego said that they looked like "somebody had grabbed him from either the front or the back using both hands and hanging on tight."[24]

The doctor concluded his comments by stating that he estimated the time of death was either late afternoon or early evening on the date the body was found, May 8.[25]

Also in evidence among the CPD files on the Shakespeare crime is a single-spaced three-page document labeled "Clinical Summary/Post Mortem Findings." As is typical of a full autopsy, every part of the body was measured, weighed, and described. Analysis of Shakespeare's body showed, just as he had always claimed, that he was indeed in very good physical shape, with most of the report's findings labeled "grossly unremarkable."[26]

(That said, a postmortem X-ray, taken by a Dr. R.J. Noveroske and included in police files, did show that Shakespeare was suffering from a "degenerative joint disease of the cervical spine." But that is a common condition that develops as people age; Shakespeare might not have even known he had it.)[27]

Well over a year after Shakespeare's murder and well after this initial report, Agent McCoy went and spoke with forensic pathologist Dr. Grant

Johnson at Memorial Hospital in Springfield. McCoy shared with Dr. Johnson crime scene and autopsy slides from the murder and the original autopsy report. Though Dr. Johnson first stated that this was only his opinion, he said his "first impression would indicate a sex motive."[28]

Johnson then went on to lament that Centralia police, upon the discovery of the body, failed to take the temperature of the corpse.[29] Had that been done, he said, an actual time of death could have been more accurately determined. Still, Johnson did go on to assert that, in his opinion, by the time John Shakespeare was found, he had already been dead for "over 24 hours."[30] Johnson based this theory on his belief that with "the towel around his head, partial decomposition would have taken place in the facial area."[31] But that had not occurred.

Later examination of the towels that had been wrapped around Shakespeare's head, meanwhile, indicated that the gun was not flush with Shakespeare's head when it was fired. Instead, it was estimated that it was probably a distance of about two feet away from the victim when the trigger was pulled.[32] Though doubtful, this does nevertheless present the possibility that the gun was fired accidentally.

After the autopsy in Centralia, the body of John Shakespeare was transferred to the city's Luer Funeral Home.[33] A local memorial service officiated by Dr. R.A. Lippman was held at the funeral home on May 11, 1975.[34] Afterward, John Shakespeare's body was transferred to Kalamazoo, Michigan, to be buried alongside his parents and other family members in that city's Riverside Cemetery. In Michigan, a graveside service for Shakespeare was held on May 12, 1975.[35]

4
THE TIMELINE

Despite the plethora of information that exists and has been uncovered about the Shakespeare murder, some basic and vital details are still unknown. For example, we do not know exactly when John Shakespeare was killed. Many accounts and most "official" records note his death date as Thursday, May 8, 1975, but that is only the day *his body was discovered*, not necessarily the day he lost his life.

For whatever reason, when Centralia police arrived at the scene, they did not take the temperature of the body.[1] Had they done so, they might have been able to narrow down this window, but without it, we are now left to speculate.

This is what we do know: Almost as soon as John Shakespeare's body was discovered (on Thursday, May 8, 1975), newspapers reported that only a few days before (on Tuesday, May 6), Shakespeare had dinner at a Centralia eatery, Pinky's, with Bill Wham and a hitchhiker who went by the name of Quinn Devon.[2] After dinner, Wham and Devon dropped Shakespeare off at his home on Pine Street at about 9:00 p.m.[3] Wham and Shakespeare had been friends for many years, and in the 1950s, Wham, an attorney, had represented Shakespeare in a legal matter with one of his car dealerships.[4]

Then, as noted, Shakespeare's body was discovered by his handyman Ralph Porter around 8:00 p.m. on Thursday, May 8, 1975.[5] In between those two days—over thirty hours—there was unaccounted-for time Shakespeare might have been alive or not.

This then presents a question: Did anyone see John Shakespeare alive after he dined with Wham and Devon?

To try to narrow this gap, police turned to Porter, the person they thought might have the most insight into Shakespeare during this period. Police sat down with Porter (who was never considered a suspect in the crime) for the first time on Thursday, May 8, 1975,[6] the day the body was discovered, and then sat down with him again, over a year later, on September 22, 1976.[7]

Frustratingly, some of Porter's recollections in the two police reports differ.

In both interviews, Porter states that the last time he spoke with—but had not laid eyes on—his boss was on Saturday, May 3, at about 3:00 p.m.[8] That day, according to Porter, Shakespeare was just leaving the house when Porter arrived. The two men spoke briefly. Shakespeare, dressed in "street clothes," told Porter that he was on his way to the local Sears and Roebuck to buy a new washer/dryer.[9]

In his original 1975 interview, Porter told police that the next time he saw—but didn't speak to—his boss was two days later (on May 5, 1975). Porter told he police that he had come over to the house to take out the trash cans and, at that time, had spotted Shakespeare through the window in the home's kitchen.[10] But in 1976, Porter said the last time he saw his boss alive he was sitting in an easy chair in the living room.[11]

In his 1975 statement, Porter said that two days after that final sighting, he again went to Shakespeare's house. This would have been Wednesday,

Opposite: The building where Pinky's Restaurant was formerly located. *Authors' collection.*

Right: The door, as it looks today, leading out of the kitchen of Shakespeare's Pine Street home; this is the side entrance. *Authors' collection.*

May 7. Porter said he arrived that day at about 7:00 p.m., and as soon as he got there, he noticed that the glass in the house's side storm door had been broken—in fact, broken outward. But, Porter said, he thought little of it; that glass had broken out before when the wind grabbed the door and slammed it too hard. Porter just made a mental note to replace the glass with the screen. Then, Porter went into the house. There Porter noticed that Shakespeare's personal set of house and car keys was lying on the kitchen table, the place where he usually left them.[12]

Then, still on that evening of the seventh, and according to his 1975 statement, Porter noticed that the kitchen light and the light in the upstairs hallway were both on. The lights were also on in the downstairs office area. Along with the lights down there, Porter also stated that he thought he had heard the sound of a typewriter coming from the basement.[13]

Or at least, that's what Porter said in 1975. In his 1976 statement, however, he amended his recollection to say that day he heard, coming up from the basement, what sounded like shoes shuffling across the floor. Porter told police he didn't think it could be Mr. Shakespeare, as Shakespeare "never wore shoes in the house."[14] But Porter, though he did say he stepped into the basement for "one to two minutes," did not investigate the noise further.[15]

The next day, Thursday, May 8, Porter returned to the house once more. Again, he arrived at about 7:00 p.m. and again went inside the home. But after that, Porter's two statements diverge. In one, he says that the upstairs lights and downstairs lights were all on, just like the day before,[16] but in the other, he says no lights were on in the upstairs though the basement lights were still burning.[17]

In any event, that evening, Porter was in need of some light bulbs for the garage (though Porter's second statement says he needed the bulbs for the hallway/stairway light). The bulbs were stored in a corner of the basement. Porter also wanted to see if the new washer/dryer had been delivered. According to him, as he headed into the basement, he called out to Shakespeare "three or four" times but received no answer. Once downstairs, Porter headed toward the back of the basement toward the furnace room where the home's washer/dryer was. In his statement to the police, Porter said, "I pulled the string to turn the light on and I saw his feet sticking out."[18]

These differences in Porter's two accounts could mean nothing—after all, human memory is far from a precise mechanism—or they could mean something.

Interior of basement in main house; note the string of hanging light fixtures across the ceiling. *Authors' collection.*

The corner of the Pine Street basement, as it looks today, where John Shakespeare's body was found in 1975. *Authors' collection.*

Perhaps the most interesting detail Porter shared (and this might be contradictory too) was about Shakespeare's keys. When he was at the house on Wednesday, Porter told police he saw Shakespeare's keys on the kitchen counter, in their "usual" place.[19] The next day, however, Porter told Detective Simon Franklin, "His keys were still hanging in the door, as if he had just opened it for someone."[20]

If this is accurate, who moved the keys? Could this mean that Shakespeare was still alive on Wednesday or even Thursday? Or had someone else been coming in and out of the house? Could someone have been in the house while Porter was actually there too? (This could then dovetail with Porter's statement of hearing footsteps in the basement.)

During the initial investigation into the crime, police had just about all but accepted as fact that Shakespeare had been dead for at least a day or maybe even several days before his body was discovered on May 8, but then a new supposed witness came forward and altered the timeline of the crime.

Not long after news of the Shakespeare murder hit the newspapers, a local man named Roscoe Meeks went to the police and claimed that he saw John Shakespeare at a local business—White's Salvage on North Beech—"around noon" on Thursday, May 8.[21] If that were true, that would mean that Shakespeare had to have been killed sometime in the afternoon or the early evening of May 8. But Meeks had a bit of a reputation around town, and many doubted his recollection. In fact, the police certainly seemed to, as shortly after interviewing Meeks, they spoke to several others (among them Bill Snell, Dick Boadright, Lee Swenson, Bill Roy, Gene Donaho, Everetts Burlison and Tom Martin) who either visited or were working at the salvage yard on the eighth, and none of those individuals recalled any sign of John Shakespeare.[22]

Still, for whatever reason, Meeks's story took hold, and many, including the police, have gone on to fully accept his version of events. Hence, almost all formal and informal records pertaining to Shakespeare's death list a death date of Thursday, May 8, 1975.

Then, confirming Meeks's story but confusing the matter even further, one of Shakespeare's neighbors, Ann Bingaman, later told police detective Rich Simer that she was "positive" she saw one of John's cars—identified by her by rust on the car's right side—being driven between 11:30 a.m. and noon on the day of the eighth. But, she elaborated, she couldn't tell who was behind the wheel.[23] Years later, however, when Simer wrote a book that dealt in part with the Shakespeare killing, he did not include Bingaman's recollection, calling into question if he considered it accurate.[24]

Despite these testimonies, other clues suggest that John Shakespeare might actually have been dead long before Thursday, May 8.

For example, in evidence at the Centralia PD is a copy of Shakespeare's final phone bill, covering the last two months of his life. Though the bill—for his number, 618-532-9436—notes only outgoing calls, it is nevertheless illustrative.[25]

Shakespeare did not seem to be a big phone talker. On this bill, there is no more than one long-distance call per day and often those calls are quite brief. Yet it is interesting that while Shakespeare made a long-distance call on Sunday, May 1, 1975, and one on Monday, May 5, 1975, not a single call was made by him on Tuesday, May 6, or Wednesday, May 7.[26] We know that Shakespeare was alive on the sixth, but could he have already been dead by Wednesday, May 7?

As is seemingly the norm in the Shakespeare case, there is contradictory evidence to this as well. In the Centralia PD files on the Shakespeare homicide, there is a handwritten note concerning an Orlando-based realtor and friend of Shakespeare's named Alvin Schubert. Contacted by police, Schubert said that he had "handled [Shakespeare's] real estate for about 13 years," and he said he spoke to Shakespeare on the phone "for about an hour Wed. night."[27]

If Schubert's recollection is true, Shakespeare's time of death has to be late on the evening of the seventh or during the day on Thursday, May 8.

But nothing in the Shakespeare case is straightforward, and the state of Shakespeare's actual home during that week in May contradicts both the seventh or eighth assumption.

For example, at the crime scene, police noted that neither Shake's daily mail (delivered via a vertical slot in the home's front door and bearing postmarks from Friday, May 2, 1975, to Thursday, May 6, 1975) nor his daily edition of the *Wall Street Journal*, which he was said to have read religiously, were opened or disturbed.[28]

Further, there is handyman Ralph Porter's aforementioned statement about the basement lights. Though Porter seems inexact about the upstairs lights, he maintained that the same basement lights were always on.[29]

Finally, there is the testimony of a local UPS driver, Lyle Robert Leckrone. Leckrone was interviewed by Agent McCoy in October 1976. He said that Shakespeare often had packages delivered to him. Usually, Shakespeare signed for them himself. But on Wednesday, May 7, when Leckrone arrived with a delivery for him, Shakespeare did not come to the side door though Leckrone knocked three times. (Leckrone also took note that the glass on the door had been busted out.) When Shakespeare didn't answer, Leckrone noticed that Shakespeare's Chevy Suburban was parked in the driveway, and he decided to just put the package in the front seat of the car. The car had been left unlocked.[30]

The next day, another delivery occurred. Leckrone noticed that the car was in the same place as it had been the day before and was still unlocked. He also saw that the package from the day before was still there. For whatever reason, Leckrone decided not to leave the second package.[31]

The recollections of Leckrone, once more, recast this crime's possible timeline. If Shakespeare was alive on Wednesday, May 7, why didn't he retrieve his package from the car? If he were driving the car on Thursday, May 8, as Ann Bingaman says, then that makes the UPS shipment still being in the vehicle even odder, especially as the Leckrone says he placed it in the front seat.

5

THE ESTATE

In some late 1973 correspondence to his then financial advisor, Albert F. Gibson, John Shakespeare ruminated on how he might like to bequeath his wealth, someday, after his passing. He wrote, "I would like my assets when I am through with them to be used to do some good for the world adn [*sic*] humanity. This might involve helping boys, through the Boy Scouts, scholarships or promoting teaching of non-Keynesian economics."[1]

But, for whatever reason, Shakespeare never set down a will.

In 1975, that lack of a will, along with Shakespeare's sudden and unexpected death, only further complicated his already complicated estate. It was soon discovered that Shakespeare had monies, stocks or investments spread out all over the world: in, among other places, the Ashland Oil Company, at the RobinsonBank in Switzerland, at the Swiss Credit Bank and in the Texaco Corporation. He even had mineral interests in some land in Daviess County, Kentucky.[2] And all of this was in addition to his remaining car collection and his White County oil field holdings and myriad other assets.[3]

Shakespeare did not, however, own his Centralian home, so that was not part of his estate.[4] The home being only "leased" to John (from a purported land trust, administered by whom?) might have been some legal maneuvering that allowed him to not have to be taxed on the home. In any event, not long after Shakespeare's death, the home was sold to a couple with the last name Hoxworth. The home has since been sold again.[5]

As mentioned previously, Shakespeare also kept a lot of money—in gold, silver and some cash—in "eight to ten bags" in hidden compartments in his home.[6] When the caches were discovered, the Centralia PD seized the stash as evidence. According to police reports, four people witnessed this exchange: Simon Franklin, Stan Pokojski, Ralph Porter and Jim Porter (Ralph Porter's thirty-nine-year-old son).[7] Usually, this sort of cache would be held at the local police department, but Centralia PD considered it too large for them to hold and, instead, entrusted it to the city's First National Bank and Trust Company to be counted and then stored. According to bank records, these assets alone totaled around $50,000 (almost $300,000 in today's money).[8] The rumor—now proven accurate—of Shakespeare hoarding wealth in his house had long been considered a possible motive for his murder. But that was not a feeling harbored by everyone—in fact, in the first article the local paper published about Shakespeare's murder, its author wondered if Shakespeare's wealth was actually "far less than many people supposed."[9]

After Shakespeare's murder, to oversee probate, Centralia attorney William B. Wham—who was also an acquaintance of Shakespeare's and had dined with him the very same week he was killed—was named as the estate's executor. For his work, Wham was paid a yearly fee of $52,000.[10]

The mid-1970s home of William Wham and family as it looks today. *Authors' collection.*

Interestingly, it would take nine years for the estate of John Shakespeare to be fully settled.

Wham must have, at least for a time, also worked with Shakespeare's surviving family members about offering a possible financial reward for information about the crime. A one-year anniversary article about the crime noted that the estate was in talks with the local Centralia bank about such an offer, but efforts were stymied by the "enormous complexity" of Shakespeare's finances.[11] (There is no evidence a reward was ever offered.)

Well over a year after his death, an auction of many of Shakespeare's personal belongings was held in Centralia. The sale, held on December 4, 1976, was administered by Centralia's First National Bank and included an odd assortment of items. Among them were navy surplus, car accessories, exercise equipment, some plywood ceiling paneling, a car hoist, steel cabinets, two "antique work cabinets," garden tools and rod iron, brass and copper fittings.[12]

Meanwhile, that same month, Ben J. Selkirk & Sons, a more high-end auction service located over in St. Louis, handled the sale of three of Shakespeare's automobiles—his Dino Ferrari GT roadster, his Type E Jaguar V-12, and the Italian Lancia four-person sedan—as well as some non-automotive items. The three cars sold for a total of just under $25,000.[13] Non-car items in the sale included a Browning shotgun, three pairs of water skis, a "spring exerciser," a Thermo-Fax copier, and an "old" IBM typewriter. Selkirk also handled the sale of various gold pieces and coins from the estate.[14]

When the estate attempted to liquidate John's overseas Monte Sole investment, however, it ran into problems.[15] It was soon discovered that the Swiss institute holding those funds was in a court-ordered receivership—and had been for several years. Though the IRS valued Shake's Monte Sole contract at over $1 million, the family obtained a payout of only $150,000, and this was achieved only after extensive international litigation.[16]

Meanwhile, the brand-new BMW that John had purchased from the foreign car firm of Schmoldt & Axman for his use in Switzerland (which he never got to drive or even take possession of) was another sticking point. Shakespeare specially ordered the vehicle, equipping it with all sorts of expensive features that most German drivers don't care about. Fearful that they wouldn't be able to resell the car, Schmoldt & Axman initially refused to refund its cost to the Shakespeare estate.[17] Finally, however, the family was able to secure a partial restitution.[18]

In the end, after a rather hefty tax bill from the IRS was paid, Shakespeare's estate was valued at around $2.3 million (which, in today's dollars, would be around $13 million).[19] As Shakespeare had no spouse or children, the funds were ultimately divided between eight of his closest relatives. Among them were his brother Henry and various nieces and nephews.[20] Henry Shakespeare received $10,000, while smaller amounts (between $2,000 and $5,000) went to Shake's other heirs.[21]

6
THE REVELATION

After twenty-five years as a resident of Centralia, as well as a member of the local Rotary Club and other civic groups, and, of course, thanks to the frequent sight of him jogging down the street in his red running shorts, John Shakespeare was a pretty well-known man about town. But there was one part of his life that he kept carefully concealed from others—that is, until after his death.

Not long following his passing, it was revealed that John Shakespeare was gay. Among the personal effects found in his home after his murder were at least one gay adult film (this was pre–home video; it was a 16mm film) as well as a copy (postmarked to him on April 1, 1975) of the California-based gay-themed catalogue the *Odyssey*, which Shake seemed to have had a subscription to.[1]

After this discovery, the fact that Shakespeare never married or was ever, to anyone's recollection, involved with a woman, suddenly made sense.[2]

In retrospect, the fact that Shakespeare remained closeted throughout his life made sense too, especially considering the time and the environs in which he lived—the latter being middle American states like Michigan, Indiana, and Illinois.

Later, some of Shakespeare's closest friends considered his sexuality an "open secret." But just how "open" is debatable. It certainly seems unlikely that, considering the times and various prejudices, any gay man, simply because he was gay, would be allowed to be a Scout leader in a small town as Shakespeare had been with the local Explorers for well for over a decade.

Again, after his death, it came to light that John might have had at least one somewhat long-term gay relationship. In the late 1940s, Shakespeare met John Schaler III in Indiana.[3] Both were car enthusiasts; Schaler was one of the foremost vendors of Rolls-Royces in the United States. Shakespeare and Shaler were also business partners at one time, selling Rolls.[4] Later, Shaler moved to Palm Beach, Florida, and worked in real estate.[5] He came to Centralia in 1975 to attend John's funeral and, while in town, phoned the CPD to offer any assistance he could.[6] Schaler died in 2004.[7]

The revelation of John Shakespeare's sexual orientation opened up new theories and suspects—with some of them nearly the polar opposites of one another.

THE GAY HOOK-UP THEORY

After local police learned of Shakespeare's sexuality, Centralia investigators did what would, today, be called "profiling." Acting on little more than local rumor and stereotypes, area police began to seek out and investigate local men who were either known to be gay or, as it says in the police notes from the time, were thought to have "homosexual tendencies." In the reports, at least four area men were mentioned by name as being among this gay group.[8]

Assumedly, these men needed to be looked into because of what has since evolved into the "Deadly Gay Hook-Up" theory in the Shakespeare murder case. Area authorities probably felt justified in pursuing this line of inquiry since, in some typed notes of a meeting that the IBI had with three high-ranking St. Louis Major Case Squad members about the case, "All three [St. Louis] detectives remarked on the strong homosexual connotations in the way the body was bound."[9]

But CPD wasn't just looking into *local* gay men.

As mentioned, found in Shakespeare's home and now among the evidence at the Centralia Police Department, was a copy of a 1975 gay-themed magazine/catalogue titled the *Odyssey*. Along with selling gay adult films and graphic posters of nude men (including those of famous porn star John Holmes), *Odyssey* was about to commence with the publishing of personal ads within its pages. These classified ads were a way for gay men to meet other gay men before the advent of things like Grindr and other social media platforms.[10]

Also in evidence at the Centralia Police Department is a neatly typed canceled check (#13678) written by Shakespeare, drawn on his local bank account and made out to "Odyssey Club" for twenty-eight dollars. The presence of this check has led to widespread speculation that, not long before his death, Shakespeare had placed a personal ad in the magazine that might have, inadvertently, invited his eventual killer(s) right into his home.[11]

But there are some problems with that theory. Shakespeare was killed in early May 1975, and his check to *Odyssey* was dated April 24, 1975, thus making the possibility of an ad making it into *Odyssey*'s pages before Shakespeare's death rather unlikely in those days of only U.S. mail. Additionally, *Odyssey*'s classified rate was $1 per line of text, and it seems unlikely that Shakespeare would have attempted to publish a twenty-eight-line personal ad.[12] Finally, a closer examination of an envelope from *Odyssey* found in Shakespeare's home, which has on it some of Shakespeare's own handwriting, suggests that he was in the process of not placing an ad but buying two 16mms (actually Super-16mm) films from the company. The merchant sold films "2 for $25," plus $3 for shipping and handling. Thus this $28 from Shakespeare seems to be fully accounted for.[13] (Also, why also would Shakespeare place such an ad when he knew he would very soon be leaving the country for an extended period?)

Still, it is possible that Shakespeare had placed an ad with *Odyssey*. But if that is true, that check has never been found. Also, it is quite possible that other gay personals existed and Shakespeare was a patron of those. It is also quite feasible that, instead of placing an ad, Shakespeare simply responded to one. However, no gay classifieds—not even those from *Odyssey*—were found among Shakespeare's papers. Further, Shakespeare's phone bill from the last two months of his life, a copy of which, as mentioned, is also in the files at the CPD, shows only a few and very short calls from him—far shorter than one would think it would take to arrange such a tryst. (Though, yes, someone could have called him, not the other way around, and those calls would not have been reflected on those bills.)[14]

If some sort of sexual encounter ultimately resulted in the death of John Shakespeare, this would then mean that Shakespeare was consensually engaging with a partner in an elaborate sex play scenario that got out of hand, resulting in Shakespeare's accidental death and then with the perpetrator(s) panicking and fleeing the scene. If this were true, it would answer the question of why no meaningful items were stolen from the Shakespeare residence (that are known of) and why Shakespeare seemed to have few (or no) marks of resistance on his body. In essence, had he been tied up, at least in the beginning, fully willingly?

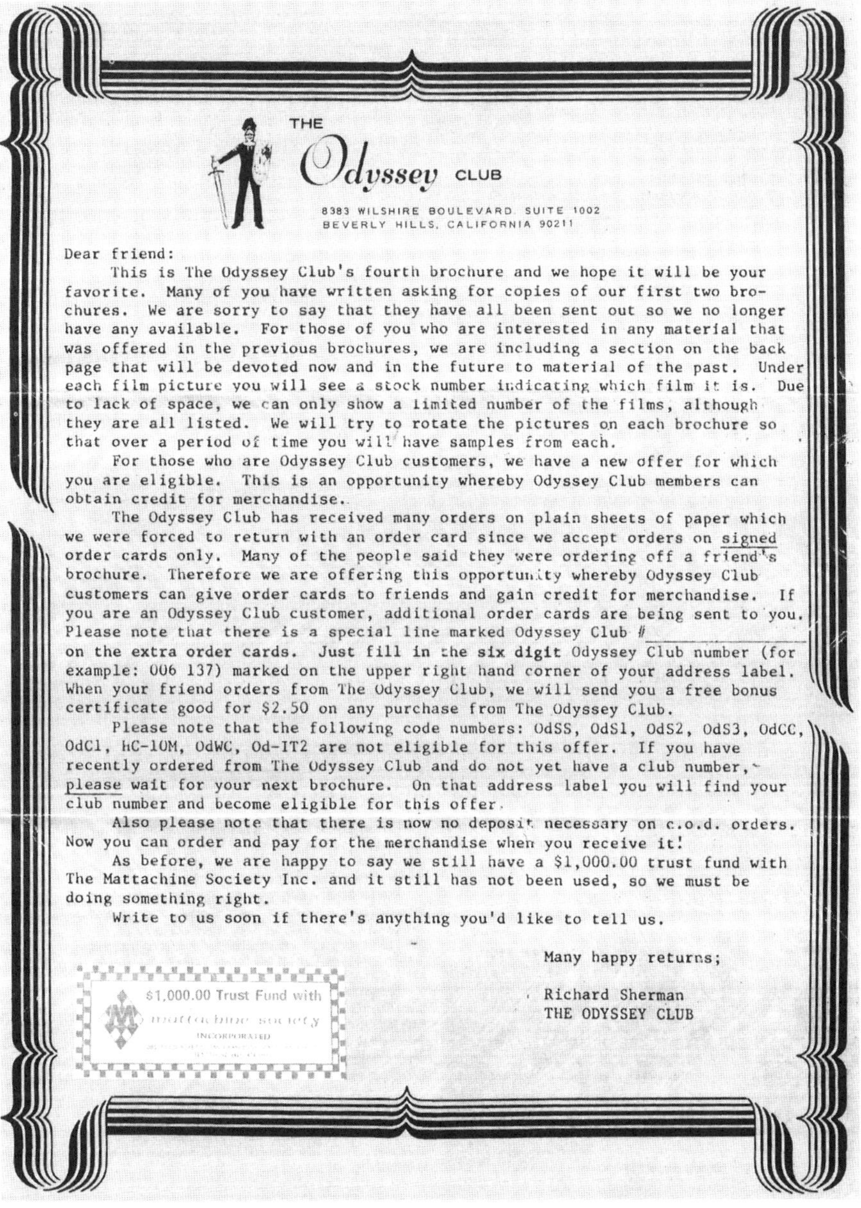

Dear friend:

This is The Odyssey Club's fourth brochure and we hope it will be your favorite. Many of you have written asking for copies of our first two brochures. We are sorry to say that they have all been sent out so we no longer have any available. For those of you who are interested in any material that was offered in the previous brochures, we are including a section on the back page that will be devoted now and in the future to material of the past. Under each film picture you will see a stock number indicating which film it is. Due to lack of space, we can only show a limited number of the films, although they are all listed. We will try to rotate the pictures on each brochure so that over a period of time you will have samples from each.

For those who are Odyssey Club customers, we have a new offer for which you are eligible. This is an opportunity whereby Odyssey Club members can obtain credit for merchandise.

The Odyssey Club has received many orders on plain sheets of paper which we were forced to return with an order card since we accept orders on signed order cards only. Many of the people said they were ordering off a friend's brochure. Therefore we are offering this opportunity whereby Odyssey Club customers can give order cards to friends and gain credit for merchandise. If you are an Odyssey Club customer, additional order cards are being sent to you. Please note that there is a special line marked Odyssey Club # ________ on the extra order cards. Just fill in the **six digit** Odyssey Club number (for example: 006 137) marked on the upper right hand corner of your address label. When your friend orders from The Odyssey Club, we will send you a free bonus certificate good for $2.50 on any purchase from The Odyssey Club.

Please note that the following code numbers: OdSS, OdS1, OdS2, OdS3, OdCC, OdC1, HC-10M, OdWC, Od-IT2 are not eligible for this offer. If you have recently ordered from The Odyssey Club and do not yet have a club number, please wait for your next brochure. On that address label you will find your club number and become eligible for this offer.

Also please note that there is now no deposit necessary on c.o.d. orders. Now you can order and pay for the merchandise when you receive it!

As before, we are happy to say we still have a $1,000.00 trust fund with The Mattachine Society Inc. and it still has not been used, so we must be doing something right.

Write to us soon if there's anything you'd like to tell us.

Many happy returns;

Richard Sherman
THE ODYSSEY CLUB

Page from the *Odyssey* catalogue; this page and others were found in Shakespeare's home after his murder. *Authors' collection.*

However, it cannot be assumed that just because Shakespeare was gay and watched adult films he partook in these sorts of casual sexual encounters. Nor can we assume that he was involved in the S&M and bondage scene. After his death, no S&M paraphernalia was found among his belongings.

Still, the CPD certainly leaped to certain assumptions. In a report from May 14, 1975, Dr. Cesar Gallego, who performed Shakespeare's autopsy, was asked by police about various S&M practices specifically as they might relate to Shakespeare's murder.[15]

Regardless of how Shakespeare might have met his killer(s), if Shakespeare's death was the result of a consensual sex act, wouldn't it have made sense for him to be nude rather than still being in his running shorts? And why is this man, almost seventy years old, in the boiler/laundry room of his basement as opposed to, say, his bedroom? Additionally, the positioning of the body, lying on his right side on the cement—though some have argued that he just "fell that way" from a standing position—suggests Shakespeare was already recumbent by the time he was tied up.

But if Shakespeare's death was *not* an accident that occurred during a mutually agreed-on sexual encounter, could it then be a criminal act where killers or thieves, using classified ads or some other type of coded or underground communication, preyed on gay men? (See chapter 8, "The Suspects," specifically its discussion of Quinn Devon.)

With so many gay men completely closeted at that time, it did leave them quite vulnerable to exploitation and blackmail. Often, after being victimized in this sort of crime, many gay men of the era (and before and after) remained fearful of then reporting these incidents to the police for fear of being ignored, ridiculed or "outed" within their own communities.

But if John Shakespeare met his demise via this manner, we are still left with the same perplexing questions that haunts almost all our theories surrounding his death: if this was a theft, why was more not stolen? And if the plan all along was to kill Shakespeare, why was he tied up in the first place?

THE HATE CRIME

That fact that John Shakespeare was known or suspected to be a closeted gay man living in 1975 in a small Midwestern town, of course, opens up another possibility for what happened to him. Was this a hate crime before we had the phrase "hate crime"?

Was the fact of being a gay man in America at that time all the justification that was needed for a man to be murdered? Sadly, history is full of accounts of men and women being killed for nothing more.

If this is true, it might actually shed light on why Shakespeare's home wasn't ransacked for valuables: the killers didn't come to the Shakespeare house to get rich but to make Centralia a town with "one less queer."

THE ANGRY DAD SCENARIO

Along these same lines, since his death in May 1975, a popular theory behind the reason Shakespeare was killed has been labeled "The Angry Dad Scenario."

Though, as mentioned earlier, there is absolutely no evidence that John Shakespeare was ever inappropriate with children, it has not stopped people from making posthumous assumptions about him. The fact that he was involved with a local Explorers group for so long has also, for some people, set off alarm bells. But to date, no former Scout member has come forth with any allegations. In fact, as mentioned in this book's first chapter on Shakespeare's life, former Scouts from his troop, when interviewed recently, had nothing but glowing things to say about Shakespeare, their former troop leader.

Still, people wonder. Did someone—be it founded in fact or not—make an accusation or have suspicion about Shakespeare that caused a local parent or, really, anyone, to, in turn, then confront John Shakespeare with these allegations and then exact immediate revenge?

That Shakespeare's head and face were covered when he was shot bespeaks of someone who might have known Shakespeare before this fateful night but who just couldn't bring themselves to look at his face as they pulled the trigger. This theory would also, once again, explain the lack of items stolen from the home. But would it explain the utter lack of bruises or other physical evidence on Shakespeare's body?

Over the years, the matter of John Shakespeare's sexuality has generated a litany of other theories, not just the aforementioned.

For example, in the intervening years, almost every one of Shakespeare's male friends and acquaintances has seen their sexual preferences speculated on as if that thereby implies that they were somehow involved in Shakespeare's death. As crime theorists follow this logic, the scenarios then become everything from "Shakespeare was romantically/sexually involved with one of them and threatening to out them!" to "Shakespeare was threatening to break up with them and was killed by this jilted lover!"

The role that Shakespeare's *Odyssey* magazine subscription and his connection to it might have played in his death have also long been theorized on, as well with a variety of tentacle-like—and one could say, far-fetched—hypotheses.

A case in point: During this period, while the LA-based *Odyssey* magazine was being printed and shipped—as clandestinely as possible, since shipping "pornography" through the U.S. mail was an arrestable offense then—there was also something called the Odyssey Foundation that *might* have been connected to it.

The Odyssey Foundation was based in San Diego, among other cities, and was operated by a man named John Paul Norman. Its rather classy name hides a horrific operation. The purpose of the Odyssey Foundation was the sex trafficking of young boys to (usually) wealthy male clients located not only all over the country but also throughout the world. The so-called Foundation maintained a complex system of communications and logistics and, quite disturbingly, served a large clientele. At its peak, it was said to have five thousand "members" and to be grossing well over $300,000 a year.[16]

Notorious serial killer John Wayne Gacy. A connection? *Authors' collection.*

John Norman was eventually caught for his crimes. But while awaiting trial in California, he ran off to Chicago and started a new, but highly similar, operation called the Delta Project. Among other nefarious activities and connections, Norman is believed to have had ties to notorious Chicago-area serial killer John Wayne Gacy.[17]

Gacy has been floated as a suspect in this crime as well. But the oldest known victim of his crimes was twenty-two years old, so him being interested in Shakespeare does not fit his modus operandi.[18] But could Gacy have been drawn to Shakespeare due to Shakespeare's Explorer involvement? (Interestingly, for a short time, Gacy had a more solid connection to Centralia. In the 1980s, a Centralian woman named Sue Terry began to correspond with Gacy while he was in prison. This pen-pal relationship eventually turned romantic, and Terry later stated that she and Gacy were engaged. Her shocking story made her a popular guest on the TV talk shows of the era, where Terry steadfastly maintained that Gacy was innocent of his crimes. Later, however, she broke off their relationship and recanted her earlier defense of him.[19] Afterward, she moved from Centralia and settled in Vermont. She died in 2006.)[20]

If a possible connection between John Norman and Gacy was not tawdry enough, then there's also the matter of a nightclub named the Odyssey Club. It was based in LA and primarily catered to gay and lesbian youth. It was owned by a man named Eddie Nash. Though this nightclub might have been legit, Nash was not, and he had a long criminal history that included drug dealing, money laundering and, possibly, even acts of arson. In 1981, he entered the true crime lexicon when he was said to have been the one who ordered the Wonderland Murders, a notorious slaughter of four people in an LA drug house.[21] (The Wonderland Murders would go on to serve as the inspiration for several films, including 1997's *Boogie Nights*.)

The Wonderland Murders also involved male porn star John Holmes. In fact, Holmes was at one time arrested and tried for the crime but was acquitted.[22] As mentioned earlier, John Holmes was *the* star talent for *Odyssey* magazine, the aforementioned producer and seller of male pornography that Shakespeare subscribed to. (Later, Eddie Nash would be arrested and tried for the Wonderland Murders, but he, too, would be acquitted.)[23]

While the connections between these men and these organizations to the Shakespeare case are rather flimsy, many who have examined the Shakespeare crime have found enough to put together the theory that they are all, somehow, linked together. Among the allegations: that Shakespeare was, via his *Odyssey* subscription, somehow embroiled in some of the lurid criminal practices of these various "Odysseys."

But as intriguing as all this might be, many of the details of these connections are pretty hard to overcome or make fit. Consider: a man named Richard Sherman was the creator *Odyssey* magazine and was based out of Beverly Hills. The Odyssey Foundation, however, was the creation of John David Norman, and it was based out of San Diego. Admittedly, both men often used aliases, but Beverly Hills and San Diego are over two hours away from each other. If they were connected or one in the same, why the distance? Additionally, for what it's worth, the Odyssey Club nightclub didn't open its doors until 1976, the year after John Shakespeare was killed.

Further, lest we forget, again there is *no evidence* that John Shakespeare was interested in little boys or advertised for them. Nor is there any evidence that he ever did anything with the *Odyssey* catalogue beyond ordering, it seems, some 16mm films to watch in the privacy of his own home.

Odyssey Foundation founder John David Norman was arrested many times over the years but somehow kept eluding any long-term jail sentence—that is, until in 1987 in Illinois, when he was arrested for the last time and was finally convicted. He spent the rest of his life behind bars and died in 2011.[24]

Eddie Nash died in 2014.[25]

The Wonderland Murders are still considered an unsolved crime.[26]

7
THE INVESTIGATION

Homicides were far from common in the city of Centralia. The killing of John Shakespeare, and the investigation of it, was unlike anything they had ever seen before.

Hundreds upon hundreds of police man-hours would eventually be devoted to trying to solve the crime. As one of the many investigators from over the years said, "We knocked on every door of the south side of town."[1]

The investigation would also eventually reach far beyond the city limits. It extended to the northern part of the state as well as to North Carolina, Florida, Colorado, California, Kentucky, Missouri, and Nebraska. (In Nebraska, two criminals who had committed similar crimes were looked into but ultimately dismissed.)[2] The investigation also went international, since Shakespeare had business interests in Switzerland and the Bahamas, among other locales.[3] For those investigations, the Centralia and Illinois police turned to assistance from both the FBI and Interpol.[4]

As early as May 9, 1975, one day after Shakespeare's body was found, a Sergeant Holmes of the Illinois State Police called Centralia Police Chief Franklin and offered his and his department's assistance with the case.[5]

Soon after, CPD contacted Special Agent James McCoy of the Illinois Bureau of Investigation to request his help in investigating the Shakespeare murder.[6]

For at least the next two years, Centralia's Simon Franklin and the IBI's Jim McCoy would be the lead investigators for this crime, following up on hundreds of leads and interviewing dozens of witnesses and suspects.

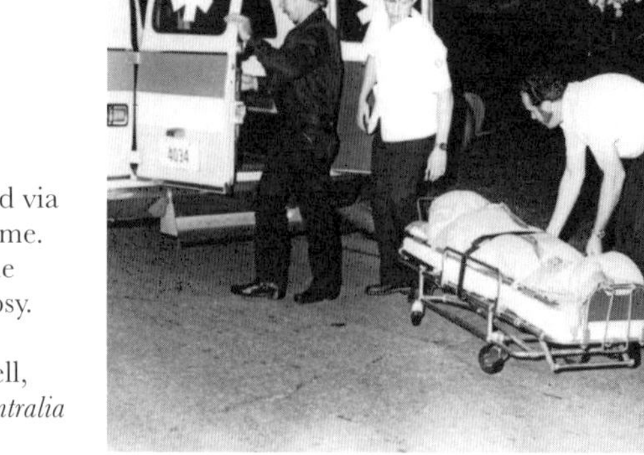

The body of John Shakespeare is removed via the side door of his home. It would be taken to the local hospital for autopsy. *From left to right*: Harry Berger, Roger Campbell, and Don Reynolds. *Centralia Police Department.*

Not surprisingly, the day that John Shakespeare's body was found, police contacted Shake's closest relative, his younger brother, Henry, who was living in Florida. Henry arrived in Centralia within days to begin the process of claiming his brother's body, settling his estate and seeing to John's eventual burial in Michigan.[7]

The day after Shakespeare's body was found, officers went to the Shakespeare home to search the autos that he had stored in his garage—the silver-gray Jaguar, the black and red Ferrari, among others—to see if they could uncover any articles, names, scraps of paper or receipts to aid in their investigation.[8]

From the beginning of the police investigation into the murder, one vital element was missing: a motive. In the press, police repeatedly bemoaned that they could not figure out a motive in this case. As Kermit Justice said, "If we knew their motive, it would help us know a direction to go."[9]

Regardless, the day after the homicide, in the press, the police were already dismissing burglary as a possible reason for the killing. According to them, with nothing of great value taken from the home, how could it be robbery?

Subsequently, IBI officials reached out to the top detectives of the St. Louis Police Department, and they, too, dismissed robbery as a motive; a robber would, they said, have made a much bigger mess of the place.[10]

But could thieves have been hoping to extort information from a tied-up Shakespeare about hidden monies or other valuables in the house? The town had long been rife with rumors that Shakespeare had cash hidden in his home (which might have been enough to entice someone to commit this crime). Did Shakespeare refuse to give up any information about this, ultimately leading to his death? But if this is what occurred, wouldn't Shakespeare's body have shown more marks of abuse or torture?

It should be noted, however, that Shakespeare's home was not out in the country somewhere, but in a normal city neighborhood with the frequent comings and goings of others. Could the invaders that night have heard something from outside the house and gotten spooked, from the sound of a car going by to a siren in the distance, making it then necessary for them to flee without any cash or other loot?

Be that as it may, if the Shakespeare homicide did not begin as a robbery, the police were still left with another deeply puzzling question: If the plan all along was to kill John Shakespeare, then why did the killer(s) go to the trouble of handcuffing him, tying him up, and covering his face and head?

Early on, Police Chief Franklin wondered aloud if this might have been a "revenge-type thing."[11] Very quickly into their investigation, police determined that they were probably looking for more than one killer. Though a gun is a great equalizer, it seemed impossible for only one person to have carried out this crime. There was no way to keep a gun on Shakespeare *and* tie him up and handcuff him. This had to be the work of at least two.[12]

After the autopsy results were returned, detectives took note of the ligature marks on Shakespeare's wrists and ankles. They might be because the handcuffs and ankle bindings were so tight or they might indicate that, at some point, Shakespeare tried to free himself. Common sense would tell us that a victim does not try to break free of their restraints while their assailant or assailants are standing over or near them. This, then, presents a brand-new question: Just how long was John Shakespeare tied up before he was killed? Humanely, we would like to think it was just seconds or minutes that Shakespeare had to endure this bondage, but no one knows for sure. Shakespeare could very well have been tied up and bound to that pipe in the basement for hours, maybe even days. His captor or captors could have left him down there while they returned to the upstairs of the house looking for something, or they might have even left the home and the property at one time before returning later to kill their victim.

That anyone got into Shakespeare's home at all was interesting. In many ways, Shakespeare had made his home into a mini fortress. About twelve years prior to his death, after his Centralia home had been robbed by a thief who broke a window, Shakespeare installed elaborate new security window frames that required a key to be opened even from the inside.[13]

Additionally, he installed doors that locked immediately when you shut them.[14] (It may have been around this time, too, that John had Ralph Porter create the secret ducts and cubbyholes in the house that eventually hid gold and silver rations, coins, and currency.)

Shakespeare was said to always be conscious—even vigilant—of locking his house's doors whenever he left home, even if he was just going to get something out of his car.[15] In a statement he gave to police, Shakespeare's handyman Ralph Porter said about the night of the murder, "The house was all locked-up—the windows are all sealed, there is no way you can get into the house without a key."[16]

But even the most enduring of habits can sometimes fail. Again, according to Porter, on warm days, Shakespeare would sometimes leave the side door

One of the fake ducts—as it looks today—in the basement of Shakespeare's Pine Street home where he hid money and other valuables. *Authors' collection.*

of his home ajar to let in the breeze. Could the door had been left open, thus giving the killers easy entry? According to weather records, on May 8, 1975, the temperature in Centralia, Illinois, was seventy-seven degrees.[17]

The police later recorded in their reports that there were no signs of forced entry.[18]

Of course, if Shakespeare knew the killer or killers, he could very well have let in his own murderer(s).

The morning after the murder, the Centralia PD, and their associates, conducted the first of the many interviews they would perform. Not surprisingly, the first of the discussions they had was with Ralph Porter, Shakespeare's handyman of the last twenty years.

It doesn't seem Porter was ever considered much of a suspect in the murder. After all, it was he who phoned the police. Additionally, Porter was the one who alerted the police to all the gold and silver hidden in the house. If not for him telling them that, no one might have ever known. Additionally, though Shakespeare was about to leave for an extended stay in Switzerland, there is no evidence that he was pulling up stakes from Centralia or terminating Porter's employment. After all, Shake never had before; amid all of his travels, he had never suspended Porter's salary. And Shakespeare did travel often. In fact, according to Porter, Shakespeare often left the country without even telling him, not even so much as a goodbye. But Shakespeare always came back and life just resumed as normal.[19]

Still, as the man who found the body, Porter and his family endured many years of public interest and scrutiny that often bordered on harassment. And at least one time, Porter did visit the home of a local attorney, Eddie Veltman.[20]

In his statement to the police, Porter recounted how many years he had worked for Shakespeare and his final interactions with him (see chapter 4, "The Timeline").

In his interview, Porter also made some interesting revelations. He stated point-blank that it was a neighbor, Bernie Gross, who killed Shakespeare.[21] He also noted the sudden appearance of a half-empty Pepsi bottle sitting on the counter in the kitchen.[22] Then, during the brief time he was in the basement and discovered the body, Porter told police that he observed an oily footprint on the floor. The oil was supposedly supplied by a shallow pan of it that was kept there. (Why there was a pan of oil in the basement is not noted; was Shakespeare working on a mechanical project or a small engine?) But who that print belonged to and why it wasn't photographed and more vigorously investigated are some of the many questions that still linger over this homicide and its investigation.[23]

In time, police would seek out and interview Shakespeare's neighbors, friends and various business associates.

John Mays was a longtime friend of Shakespeare's and a fellow race car enthusiast. He lived in Florida and seemed to have spoken to investigators early on, though the notes of his interview are undated. Police determined that, ultimately, Mays had little to add to their case. But Mays did say that John was always hesitant to keep too much gold in his home, as he felt this would make him too much of a magnet for robbery. (Then, in a half-pursued line of questioning, the police also asked Mays if he knew if Shakespeare had a fear of enclosed spaces. Mays said he did not.)[24]

In October 1976, former Explorer Scout Bob Magnan was interviewed by police.[25] He told police he had seen a Jaguar sometimes parked at the Shakespeare home late into the evenings.[26] That Jaguar was later believed to have belonged to a man named William Flanigan (see chapter 8, "The Suspects"). Magnan later also reported to police that he had seen a variety of motorcycles around Shakespeare's home. This might not be anything significant, as late in his life, Shakespeare did begin to develop an interest in motorcycles.[27]

Magnan was also questioned about other facets of John Shakespeare. Magnan disclosed that he had known Shake for about ten years, having met him through the Explorers troop. He and his friend Pat Stedelin had seen Shakespeare only days before Shakespeare was killed. They bumped into him briefly on the street and discussed with him an upcoming Explorer trip to the Current River in Missouri.[28]

Police also asked Magnan if he was familiar with Shakespeare's habits regarding locking his cars. Magnan said Shakespeare never left his green Chevy Suburban unlocked. Magnan also said he had driven the car many times, always with the permission of Shakespeare, but first, he had to have him unlock it.[29]

Police also asked Magnan if he ever saw a pair of handcuffs at Shakespeare's house. He had not. They asked him if he ever saw a gun. Magnan said he had not seen a gun either.[30]

Finally, police asked Magnan about that green Jaguar. Magnan described the car as being in "bad shape" and the driver as being about 5'10", 180 pounds, wearing glasses, with a goatee and gray hair.[31]

Magnan concluded his interview by saying he had been hanging out with his friend Pat Stedelin all day on May 8, 1975, but couldn't remember exactly where. (This interview, however, did occur more than a year after the fact.) He said that, on the night of the eighth, he arrived back in town around 10:00 p.m. just as police, an ambulance, and a crowd of people gathered around the Shakespeare residence.[32]

Quite some time later, in October 1976, police spoke with Vince and Ruth Sindelar. By then, the Sindelars were living in Arkansas, but they had lived near Shakespeare in Centralia in 1975. They said they had known the victim for fifteen years. The Sindelars said the last time they saw Shakespeare was about two weeks before his murder. They said that Shakespeare was known to always keep his car locked.

Ruth Sindelar also mentioned that she once spoke to a neighbor of hers, Gene Reynolds, and he claimed to have seen a car pull out of Shakespeare's driveway "a day or two before the victim was found dead."[33]

Another neighbor, Lynn Neidecker, reported seeing a "tall slim man" in Shakespeare's backyard on May 5.[34]

As late as November 1976, Agent McCoy chatted with Don Vonderhiede, also a neighbor of Shakespeare's. Vonderhiede stated he recalled seeing Shakespeare walking south on Poplar Street only a few days before his murder. Later, he recalled that he had seen two sports cars "sitting in Shakespeare's driveway the week before the body was found." Vonderhiede described the two vehicles as being an "old foreign rag-top in pretty bad shape" and a possible "greyish-brown" Jaguar.[35]

That same month, Agent McCoy also talked with Karen Meadur, a onetime neighbor of Shakespeare's. She was living near him in May 1975 and reported seeing an unfamiliar car on the 500 block of Cedar. She said that for two nights in a row, around the time that Shakespeare was killed, the same man got out of that car, walked to Sixth Street and then west on Sixth and then walked back the same way. On both nights, she said, the man arrived at around 11:00 p.m.[36]

In keeping with the time-honored adage that the criminal always returns to the scene of the crime, police paid special attention to those who gathered outside the house the night the body of John Shakespeare was found. Among those spotted at the Shakespeare house were Lee Hanon, Bernie Gross, John J. Shaler Jr., and Gene Reynolds, along with Explorer Scout Bob Magnan. (Magnan reported most of the other names to the police.)[37]

On May 11, a memorial service was held for John Shakespeare at the Luer Funeral Home in Centralia. The police also wanted to see who attended the Shakespeare service. Somewhat surprisingly, Centralia police have in their possession the original guest book from the memorial. It was either never sent to the family or the police asked to retain it. In any event, from the book, it appears that over eighty people came to pay their last respects to John. While some of the signatures are illegible, other names are discernible and are not surprising—David Agee, members of the Wham family, longtime Shakespeare friend John Schaler, Mr. and Mrs. Lee Hanon, and Ralph Porter. Others who signed: Chris Conway, Judith Joy, Mr. and Mrs. Curtis Fark, Frank Davidson, Mr. and Mrs. Bill Newman, Steve Hill (BSA/1st Class), Sandra Swanson, Roger Watwood, Marilyn Fields, George Owens, Paul Carpenter, Mr. and Mrs. David Morse, and the parents of many of the Explorer Scouts Shake had mentored over the years.[38]

Centralia police also have photocopies of the pages from the memorial book from the Kalamazoo service for Shakespeare in Michigan a few days later. This book also includes a typed list of flower arrangements sent to the cemetery; among the well-wishers were Mary Keenan, Kitty and Steve Prewhella, Tom and Laura Holewa, Jane and Roger Edwards, Steve and Neta Chappell, and Robert Jeska and family.[39]

Without any solid motive evident in this crime, police decided that the most expedient way to try to solve it was to locate the gun that the killer(s) used: If they could find the gun, they could, hopefully, find who pulled the trigger.

When sent for forensic testing, the "slug" removed from John Shakespeare's head was described as having "six lands and grooves."[40] But investigators wondered how conclusive they could be with this piece of evidence.

Repeatedly, the bullet was described as "partially flattened."[41] Still, the investigators wanted to follow up on every lead they had.

One of the first firearms they investigated came to them when an abandoned .22 turned up near the town of Odin, Illinois, about fifteen miles from Centralia. The gun had been discovered next to some railroad tracks on May 12, 1975, and Agent McCoy and Centralia Detective Richard Simer went to talk to the local couple who found it. According to Max and Pearl Howell, they were on their way to work when, near the tracks, they stumbled upon the gun, still partially in its holster, lying on the ground. The Howells picked it up and alerted Centralia police.[42]

Investigators were able to trace the gun back to Mann's Sporting Goods in Pinkneyville, Illinois. In November 1976, two Centralia officers traveled to Pinckneyville and spoke with that shop's owner.[43]

The gun they presented to Mann's owner was, he was sure, one that he had sold. Unfortunately, the owner could not remember who he sold that gun to, only that it was a "coon hunter from Centralia." Further examination of the weapon by Mann further suggested that the gun had, in fact, been used in hunting.[44]

The firearm found in Odin, Illinois (serial number: 148263), seemed to be the one that police were most interested in for a time. Obviously, the type, timing and locale of this "lost" gun is interesting: a discarded .22 found so close to Centralia? A theory soon developed that whoever had the gun had attempted to get rid of it by throwing it onto a moving train car. But while that is feasible, why that method of disposal? Even a speeding train will eventually have to stop somewhere, and the area around Centralia presents acres upon acres of empty fields, as well as abandoned structures and numerous lakes and ponds that could be used to conceal a gun.

Having the Odin gun in their hands, however, did not stop detectives from exploring other options in relation to finding the possible murder weapon. In fact, for the next several years, the investigators working the Shakespeare case would travel far and wide to track down firearms that they thought might have helped them close the case. For example:

- A man named Cecil Perkins allegedly stole a shotgun from a sporting goods store in 1974. Police tried—but failed—to track him and the gun down.[45]
- David Hatley, another hitchhiker to the city of Centralia in 1975 (see chapter 8, "The Suspects"), had a gun in his

possession. It was later confiscated and tested, but the results proved inconclusive.[46]

- In early June 1975, James McCoy traveled to the Bureau of Alcohol, Tobacco and Firearms office in Missouri. He hoped they could trace yet another .22 that he was seeking for comparison.[47]
- In August 1976, Centralia officers traveled to Pinckneyville again to speak to the owner of Hicks Trading Station about a gun he might have sold. But the owner of that store, Dale Hicks, could not trace the gun back through the records and could not confirm that he sold it.[48] Nevertheless, this asks a question: What gun was this?
- In 1983, Detective Simer went to the offices of the local newspaper, the *Centralia Sentinel.* He wanted to review the want ads that ran in the paper during the months of November and December 1974 and January and February 1975. He hoped to come across an ad offering to sell a .22.[49]

Eventually, via the newspaper, the police found two gun-related ads that ran in the classifieds in January of '75. By using the local city directory, they then sourced them back to the sellers. Following the trail of one, police interviewed Keith Meredith, who recalled selling a gun for fifty-five dollars to a man whose last name began with "G." Police later promised to return to show Meredith a photo of a man named David Gaddy.[50] (See "The Suspects" chapter.)

Then, in 1983, a Springfield, Illinois man, Timothy Crumpler, was murdered, and this crime had some similarities to the Shakespeare killing. Wondering if there might have been a connection, James McCoy had the Shakespeare bullet compared to the one that killed Crumpler. But test results showed that the two bullets "could not have been fired from the same weapon."[51]

Finally, a Centralia officer, the late Arland Speidel, gave an intriguing interview to a newspaper. Though its text endures, the title, source, and date do not. In it, Speidel mentions a gun procured at a Western Auto store in Pinkneyville that could not be traced back to anyone. He says further that it was then placed in storage by the CPD, and he believed it was later sold as police surplus inventory. Again: What gun was this? Was it the same as the Hicks Trading Post gun?[52]

And is Speidel's comment about it being sold at auction accurate? Though police auctions often include cars, bikes, and all sorts of electronic equipment, listing guns among the items up for sale is not usual.

In the end, at least four guns were acquired and tested by police specifically in relation to the Shakespeare case. None of them were believed to be the gun that fired the bullet that killed John Shakespeare.

It further seems that two of these guns, after being test-fired, must have been returned to their owners, but—and despite various rumors to the contrary—two guns (probably the one from Odin and the one that belonged to David Hatley) are still in the collection of evidence at the Centralia police headquarters.

Being unable to locate the gun, authorities then turned to other pieces of evidence from the crime scene. When Shakespeare was found, two large beach towels had been wrapped around his head. The towels were believed to have belonged to Shakespeare, which would not be surprising for a man who enjoyed water skiing and scuba diving.

The presence of those towels and why they were used has, throughout the history of this investigation, been a frequent topic of debate.

Were the towels there so that whoever pulled the trigger wouldn't have to look at his victim's face? Or were the towels there for more practical, if gruesome, reasons—to muffle any screams Shakespeare might make or to prevent a bloody backsplash when the gun went off?

The towels were later examined at the IBI labs in Springfield, Illinois. Notably, each had been tied in a knot. But according to the forensic report, only one of the towels contained a bullet hole. Sadly, no other useful information was procured from the towels at that time.[53]

Police also looked at the long yellow extension cord that bound John's body to the pipe in the basement. Its origin was never proven—did it belong to Shakespeare or was it brought to the house by his killer(s)? Considering Shakespeare's love of tinkering and working with electronics, it would be highly plausible that the cord belonged to him. The analysis of the yellow cord did bring with it two interesting facts. First, the cord had several knots tied in it, knots described as being of the "square" or "reef" type,[54] usually associated with military use.[55] And then, the way the knots were tied also indicated to investigator Mike Geurin that whoever tied them had to be left-handed.[56]

Finally, the handcuffs. Where did those come from?

Shubert Fox, a friend of Shakespeare's, later told police that he had once seen a pair of handcuffs in John's house, but they were old and tarnished; the ones from the crime scene seemed new.[57]

In late 1976, Detective Simer reached out to the Smith & Wesson company in Springfield, Massachusetts. He was hoping to trace the handcuffs. But other than the serial number from the cuffs (#039180), the company had little to go on. In December of '76, they wrote back to Simer and said, "The serial number which is stamped on the handcuffs is for the convenience of law enforcement and is not a registration number by which we record shipment."[58] As Detective Franklin later lamented, "There could be thousands or more with the same number."[59]

(Later, in the press, Simon Franklin stated definitively that the cuffs *did not* belong to Shakespeare, but he did not elaborate on how the police determined that, adding only, "It's confidential.")[60]

The cuffs also yielded no fingerprints.[61]

The provenance of all these items—from the cuffs to the cord to the cloth, possibly torn from a man's shirt and used to bind Shakespeare's ankles—has long been a quandary for law enforcement. If the killer(s) had planned to tie up Shakespeare all along, why did they not bring their own tools—for example, their own rope—rather than assume that these items could be found at the Shakespeare residence? This then leads to other questions: Did they not expect Shakespeare to be at home? Or did they, originally, have no plan to subdue him? Or had they been in the house before and knew where these various articles were located?

After his death, a hair sample was taken from Shakespeare's head. A few days later, on the hunt of a mysterious hitchhiker, Quinn Devon, who had arrived in Centralia only days before Shakespeare's death, hairs were also collected from the home of Centralian attorney William Wham, at whose house the hitchhiker had stayed for one night.[62] (See chapter 8, "The Suspects.")

These hairs, sometimes described as light brown or even blond in color, were also sent for analysis.[63] But with nothing to compare them to, they have (so far) proved of little use in the investigation.

Similar findings—or non-findings—were also returned on the two rags at the crime scene, one of which had been wrapped about Shakespeare's neck and is believed to have been a gag that Shakespeare was able to free himself from.[64]

Today, the handcuffs, the yellow extension cord, and the bloody towels are all still in evidence at the Centralia Police Department. Also in their

Centralia Police Station and City Hall as it looks today. *Authors' collection.*

possession: the wristwatch Shakespeare was wearing when he was killed (odd that the killer[s] didn't bother to take that), two clear plastic bags with hair samples from the two homes, and the two handguns.

Also spread among the three banker's boxes of physical evidence at the police station are other personal odds and ends of Shakespeare's: some business and membership cards, some personal correspondence and greeting cards, one 8mm film that was privately purchased and is probably adult in content, three rolls of home movie–type film (it is unknown what is on these films), and a vial of John Shakespeare's blood taken from him at his autopsy.[65]

Lest we forget, forensic testing was not as developed in 1975 as it is today. Hence, without those later scientific developments, it was not possible for this physical evidence to yield as much information as it could if found today.

Instead, police were forced to fall back on old-fashioned police work—the interviewing of everyone and anyone who had ever done business with John Shakespeare or knew John Shakespeare, or anyone who might have something (no matter how slight and seemingly insignificant) to gain by his murder. In their canvassing of all these associates and possible associates and suspicious strangers, again, the CPD and the IBI cast their net wide. Early in the investigation, Kermit Justice was quoted in the press as saying, "At this point, everybody is a suspect."[66]

8
THE SUSPECTS

Centralia is a small town. And John Shakespeare, a twenty-five-year resident, seemed to have a good reputation. Even one of the lead detectives investigating his murder said, "Everyone seems to have had the highest regard for him."[1] And an associate of Shakespeare's considered him a dignified and distinguished man: "John never had anything to do with any lowlifes."[2]

Still, after his May 1975 murder, a disturbing number of locals—some of whom John might well have even considered friends—were suddenly suspected of having killed him. Perhaps it was just the police doing their job, casting their net wide, to try to locate and then punish this murderer, and that's why so many people suddenly found themselves under intense scrutiny. Perhaps John Shakespeare being a wealthy man, a city "outsider" (though he'd been living there for a quarter of a century), a suspected "queer," or just a garden-variety eccentric made him an easy target for crime.

In any event, according to the records of the investigation, all of the following were, at one time or another, considered a "person of interest" in the murder of John Shakespeare.

QUINN DEVON

The name he gave was Quinn Devon (or Davon or even Devin). He has long been the main suspect in the murder. Unfortunately, no one has ever been able to find him to ask him about the murder. In fact, no one has been able to prove who he even was.

Devon was a mysterious hitchhiker who wandered into town only a few days before the murder. He might have been a killer or might just have been someone with exceptionally bad timing for having traveled through a small town only a few days before one of its most prominent citizens was found dead.

Quinn Devon—as we'll call him—arrived in Centralia via Mt. Vernon, Illinois. He also arrived due to the largesse of well-known Centralia attorney William B. "Bill" Wham.

As the story goes, Wham was doing business on May 6 up in Mt. Vernon, as was another Centralia attorney, Curt Lackey. The two men were friendly rivals in town and respected each other professionally; their offices were just down the street from each other. Wham learned that Lakey was to be in Mt. Vernon on that same day he was going to be. He suggested the two of them meet for lunch.[3]

According to Lackey, by the time he arrived at Mt. Vernon's Dutch Pantry eatery, Wham was already seated and in a "deep" conversation with a man Lackey had never seen before.[4]

When Lackey joined them, he found out why Bill was anxious to talk to this person. Wham was apparently planning a trip to Ireland in the near future, and when Wham heard this man's Irish accent, he quickly started up a chat. Lackey would later describe Wham as "a nice guy and not shy."[5]

Lackey later learned the name of the man at the table with Wham, Quinn Devon. Lackey went on to describe him as "presentable," "very intelligent," and, as far as he could tell, authentic in his accent and nationality and in his personal history. Devon shared that he was an Irishman making his way across the United States.[6]

At lunch, Wham and Devon carried on so fully that Lackey would later say he felt like a "fifth wheel," but he didn't take it personally. Just as the meal was winding up, it began to rain heavily, and rather than force his new Irish friend out into the storm, Wham offered him a ride to Centralia. Devon accepted. Meanwhile, Lackey got in his car, alone, and also left for Centralia.[7]

Recollections from Lackey, Wham and others who met Devon during his abbreviated time in southern Illinois have come together to form something of a biography of this mystery man.

According to what Devon said, he arrived in the United States by way of Florida as a stowaway on a ship then bound for South America. He had worked in restaurants as he hitchhiked his way up through Florida and Tennessee. He was an Irishman who was a journalism teacher and a writer and had once worked for the BBC. For the UK network, he had, he said, run afoul of many powerful people because of a documentary (unknown if it was for radio or television) he wrote on the Northern Ireland "Troubles." He had also spent some time in Africa, possibly teaching or writing for the BBC. There, allegedly, he married an African woman, also a teacher, but she had since passed away.[8]

When Wham and Devon arrived in Centralia, Wham showed him even more kindness. He brought Devon to his law offices (located at 212 East Broadway) and introduced him to two members of his staff.[9]

By that time, the rain had let up, and Devon wandered out of the Wham offices and down the street. He wandered first into Ritchie Camera Shop and then into a local eatery.[10] There he made the acquaintance of two other Centralia citizens, Tony "T.C." Cunningham and Mark Miller. Allegedly, Devon was talking to everyone, asking them about possible job leads.[11]

Devon and Cunningham seemed to really hit it off.

According to one report, at the Centralia diner, Devon realized he had left his backpack at Wham's legal offices. He had to return to retrieve it.[12] A different report lists Wham telling Devon to return to his office later in the day.[13]

In any event, Devon, with Cunningham and Miller now tagging along, walked back down the streets of Centralia, chatting, and they might have smoked a joint.[14] Devon allegedly even took some time to demonstrate his slick fighting moves to Cunningham.[15]

When Devon returned to Wham's East Broadway office, Wham invited him to dinner that evening with a local friend of his he thought Devon would have many things in common with. That friend was John Shakespeare.[16]

At about 5:00 p.m., Wham and Devon left the law offices and went to Wham's family home.[17] Wham had been recently widowed; his wife, Mary Alice, had passed away just one year prior. The Whams had three children; the only one still at the home—or at least the only one at home that evening—was his fourteen-year-old daughter, Jeanne.[18]

At his house, Wham offered Devon a change of clothes and even a pair of shoes to wear. They then left together and drove to Shakespeare's home to pick him up for dinner. At about 7:10 p.m., the three men sat down at Pinky's, a local restaurant located on North Oak.[19]

According to Wham, ultimately the only person ever able to be interviewed about that dinner, the three men had a nice, leisurely meal, and Wham

The exterior of the Wham legal offices in Centralia as they look today. *Authors' collection.*

reported that Shake seemed to be in good spirits.[20] They discussed Ireland, Africa, politics, economics and religion; Quinn said he was Catholic. Wham reported later that each had one mixed drink with their meal. Before leaving Pinky's, Shakespeare gave Devon the phone number of his home in Switzerland, stating that he'd be there soon, and that Devon should feel free to stop by. Notably, Wham later said that he did not recall Devon writing the number down.[21]

At about 9:00 p.m., the meal done, Wham and Devon drove Shakespeare back to his home.[22] After dropping off Shake, the two men then drove back to Wham's house, where Wham invited Devon to stay the night. Before turning in, Devon and Wham's daughter Jeanne sat in the living room watching television, with Devon drinking a Pepsi cola from the fridge and sharing stories about his life in the United Kingdom and Africa.[23]

The next morning, May 7, at around seven o'clock, per Devon's request, Wham drove Devon to a spot near the high school in the nearby town of Sandoval so that Devon could continue his trek via IL Route 50. That morning, Wham dropped him off in front of the town's high school. Devon supposedly wanted to keep the shoes that Wham had lent him, but Wham declined and gave him ten dollars instead.[24]

That was the last time anyone from Centralia ever saw or spoke to Quinn Devon.

As one can imagine, after John Shakespeare's murder was discovered on May 8, police immediately had to retrace his last few hours. And as Bill Wham and this hitchhiker were, quite possibly, among the very last people to ever see Shakespeare alive, they became key witnesses, perhaps even primary suspects.

Devon was quickly under major suspicion—a cursory review of the crime scene showed that Shakespeare's legs had been tied together with what appeared to be some cloth torn from a man's shirt—a shirt, they learned later, that looked like the one Devon had had on.[25]

Police and area law enforcement agencies moved quickly.

From Wham, they learned of the existence of this mysterious hitchhiker.[26] They also had Wham sit down with an officer to help create a composite drawing of what Devon looked like. Wham described the hitchhiker as approximately thirty-six years old, 5'8", 180 pounds, with "sandy red" hair.[27] The sketch artist also met with Jeanne Wham, Bill's teenage daughter, who had spent time with Devon and described him as about thirty to thirty-five years old and with a receding hairline of reddish-blond hair. Then the artist met with Janice Maschhoff, who worked in Wham's office, and with Sheila Jolliff, another "office girl," who had also met Devon when Wham brought him to his workplace.[28]

Today, Janice Maschhoff is Janice Seiz, and she barely remembers Quinn Devon. But she does remember going down to the police station to formulate a sketch composite.[29] She described Devon as 5'11", 180 pounds, mid-thirties and with sandy-blond hair.

(A police note from the era suggests that Cunningham and Miller were to be brought into the station to help create composite drawings, but there's no proof that either ever did.)[30]

Sheila Jolliff now Sheila Buxton however, remembers Devon, and though she wasn't surprised that Bill Wham would take pity on this vagabond and help him out so much (Mr. Wham was, she said, "nice, kind, giving"), she found the man he brought back to be "creepy."[31] That man, however, was quickly smitten with her. Buxton was just eighteen years old and had just graduated from high school; she was working that summer in Wham's office

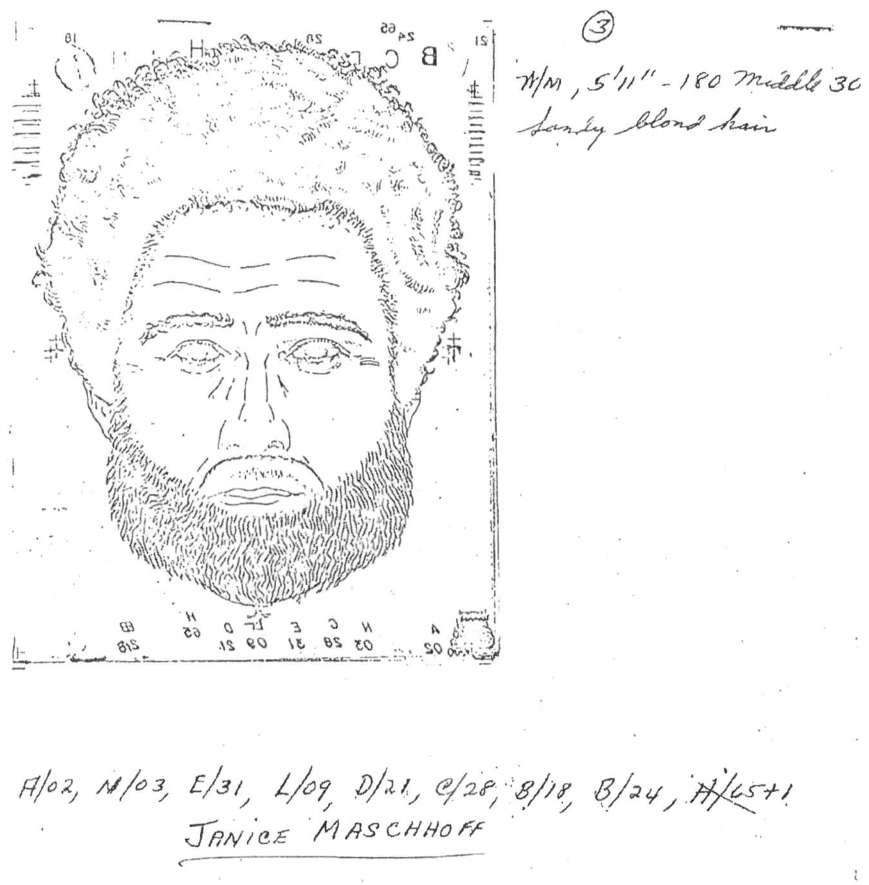

Janice Maschhoff's police-aided sketch of the mysterious "Quinn Devon." *Courtesy of the Centralia Police Department.*

and engaged to be married later in the season. She recalled, "[Devon] asked me to dinner, and I said no, and he seemed a little mad when I turned him down. Then he wanted me to take him to Sandoval the next morning, and I said no to that too. Like I said, I thought he was creepy."[32]

Jolliff noted the stranger as being of "medium" build with strawberry-blond hair and green eyes.[33] (The artist renderings of Devon are all now part of the CPD's evidence file.)

After the murder, to locate Devon, who had since left town, on May 14, 1975, Judge E. Harold Wineland of Marion County issued a material witness summons for Quinn Devon to be found, detained, and returned to Marion

County for questioning. The next day, coverage of this summons appeared in newspapers all over the Midwest.[34]

Centralia police worked to trace Devon's trail after he left the city limits. First, Devon was reported to be in Caryle, Illinois. A waitress at a Caryle eatery named Karen Clark reported to the police that Devon had come in at about 9:00 a.m. on May 7. There, she said, he ordered tea and orange juice.[35] Later that same day, he was seen by Leona Hearster, a bartender at Bill's Play House tavern.[36]

Next, he was traced to Breese, Illinois, where, hitchhiking again, he was picked up by a man named Charles Casey at about 12:30 p.m. Casey later told police that the man was wearing khaki pants, red-headed, 5'10", spoke with an Irish accent, seemed very intelligent, and was between the ages of twenty-six and thirty-six. Casey said he took the hitchhiker as far as Aviston, Illinois, and dropped him off at the Angel Haven Café. That was at approximately 1:00 p.m. on May 7.[37]

The hitchhiker was next spotted in Fairview Heights, Illinois, on Wednesday night, May 7, at a local Denny's. He was seen talking to two women and asking them for money. The two women declined but referred him to a nearby police officer who was also in the restaurant. Devon told them he couldn't talk to the cop since he was in the country illegally.[38]

After leaving Fairview Heights, Devon was reported as heading toward O'Fallon, Illinois, to the McDonald's there to see about a job.[39]

After that, he was next sighted in St. Louis and then in Columbia, Missouri,[40] and after that, he was said to be in Boonville, Missouri.[41]

When Centralia police learned of him in Missouri, they made a beeline for Columbia and then to Boonville. Centralia Detective Simon Franklin later reported in the news that "[Devon] stayed three nights with a person in Columbia. That person called the police last night after seeing Devon's name in a newspaper. The authorities checked with us and then went to the house to pick him up. But he was gone."[42]

By the time the police got to Boonville, the police had just missed Quinn Devon again. He had been staying with a woman there, but when she heard that police were looking for him, she warned him and he fled. Cops arrived just twenty minutes after he ran.[43]

That was the last sighting anyone ever had of the phantom-like Quinn Devon. But police continued to explore every angle to find him.

From Wham, they had learned that before coming to Illinois, Devon supposedly passed through Memphis, Tennessee, and obtained overnight lodging from a couple there. (Devon alleged that the couple might have also stolen some cash from him.) Police attempted to find that Memphis couple but had no luck. The CPD also contacted Memphis's Central Records Division, hunting for Devon as either complainant or victim. No records were found.[44]

Later, the IBI, which was also working the case, reached out to the Irish Consul in Chicago to see if the consulate knew of any such person. It did not. Furthermore, Irish Consular Thomas Lyons, when spoken to by police, doubted the veracity of Devon's many claims.[45]

In 1977, the police of Dublin were contacted to see if they had any knowledge of a Quinn Devon. They did not.[46]

Over the years, others have attempted to find him. Intrepid podcast host Ashley Casseday once phoned the BBC to see if they had any employment records for a Quinn Devon. They had no record of him either.[47]

In the research for this book, calls to the police departments of both Columbia and Boonville unearthed no evidence that they had ever dealt with a Quinn Devon or, for that matter, ever dealt with the Centralia PD. Newspapers in each town were also contacted, but they had no mention anywhere in their files about him. And posts on various Columbia- and Boonville-related websites and Facebook pages also yielded no information or jarred any memories. In research for this book, a private investigator had no luck turning up this mystery man either.

Obviously, "Quinn Devon" was probably not his real name. If he was in the country illegally, what is a better way to be "hidden" and untraceable than to adopt a pseudonym?

Because of the great mystery surrounding Devon, an enormous amount of speculation has grown up around him, including, among other theories, that he was a hit man hired to kill John Shakespeare. But even at the time, police discounted the "professional hit man" scenario, as a professional would never waste time tying up his victim before killing him as Shakespeare's killer did. (Though a hit man would be good at leaving behind so few clues, as this killer pretty much did.)

As Judge Ronald Niemann stated in his first interview about the case, "That doesn't rule out the possibility of a conspiracy, aiding and abetting."[48]

One of the more interesting theories about Quinn Devon is that he was really a man named Donald Kennedy Majors, a notorious killer who had a rap sheet that started back in the 1940s. Majors's career as a fugitive began when he went AWOL from the military. Soon he had warrants out for him in Wyoming, Washington, and Iowa. In Oregon, in 1958, Majors was charged with kidnapping.[49] Later, he adopted as a criminal MO locating male victims via sex-related classified ads and then robbing and/or killing them. In late 1974, that seems to be how he came to kill, by gunshot, an Oregon man named Franklin Monohan.[50]

Suspicion that Devon and Majors were the same person gained traction, due not only to the nature of his crimes but also the fact that Majors was discovered to have been in Illinois at the time of the Shakespeare murder. Additionally, Majors was described as redheaded and of Irish descent and often adopting Irish-sounding aliases, including John Patrick O'Hara. (Alas, there's no record of a "Quinn Devon.")[51]

Later, Majors once boasted that during his criminal career he had killed "33 and a half people." The "half," according to Majors, was because though he shot a man, it seemed to only knock him unconscious, not kill him. Majors's choice of weapon: a .22.[52]

But as compelling as the Majors-Devon connection seems to be, there remain some problems with it.

First, when he was arrested, Majors supposedly had in his possession a giant file of letters and notes and telephone numbers from gay men around the country who had advertised for sex, but Majors usually preyed entirely on straight men interesting in pursuing a "swinging" lifestyle. The ads that Major placed and responded to were geared almost exclusively to this part of the population. Majors would then use one or two women traveling with him—sometimes traveling unwillingly—as "bait" with these men, whom he would then either subdue and rob or kill and rob.[53]

Second, there is nothing that places Majors in or near Centralia at the time of the Shakespeare murder. Though Majors, whose murder of Monohan is detailed in Ann Rule's 2013 crime anthology *But I Trusted You*, can be placed in Illinois in 1975, he never seemed to be any farther south than Matteson, a town about thirty miles south of Chicago and a long way from Centralia.[54]

Further, Majors crisscrossed the country in a variety of vehicles—including an old Chevy—so why would he be hitchhiking? Also, Majors always seemed to travel with one or two women to use in his scheme, but Devon was alone.[55]

Then, as mentioned, Majors seemed to prey exclusively on straight men interested in the "swingers" lifestyle, not on gay men. And even if he did, if Majors was looking for wealthy gay men to rob, it's hard to believe that the Chicago area did not offer a fair share of vulnerable would-be victims for him. (Besides there's also no solid evidence that Shakespeare ever placed, or responded to, any personal ads.)

Furthermore, in 1975, Majors would have been fifty-two years old, and judging by a mug shot of him taken around that time, he looked every one of his fifty-two years. But no one who laid eyes on Quinn Devon during his brief time in and around Centralia ever described him as being that old; most witnesses reported him as late twenties or, at most, mid- to late thirties.

Finally, Majors was quite tall: police files describe him as perhaps as tall as 6'5", and Devon was never described as such.

There's also no record of Majors ever affecting a put-on accent. And remember, nothing was truly stolen from Shakespeare's home after he was killed. When Monohan died, Majors took his credit cards and used them. Why wouldn't this killing be the same?

Donald Kennedy Majors did get arrested in July 1975 and went to jail in 1978 for the Monohan murder. Even with the plea bargain that he eventually agreed to, he ended up with two life sentences.[56] He died in prison in August 2010.[57]

So then: Who was Quinn Devon? He was a real person—inasmuch as people saw him. But if his name was fake, was the rest of his story true? Notably, the early 1970s were the biggest, bloodiest years in the conflicts in Ireland. It would make sense that if the BBC was producing programs on that topic, it would have been around that time. Thus, if that's the case, it does give Devon enough time to finish the film, make his way to Africa and still be in the United States by the mid-1970s.

Authenticating any other part of his life/story has just been a long series of complete dead ends. So we are left to speculate.

Was Quinn Devon a hit man hired to take out John Shakespeare? Do hit men hitchhike? Additionally, why create such an elaborate story and persona? Why walk around town so out in the open? Why not, alternatively, arrive and exit under the cover of night? Why sit down to a meal and be seen directly opposite the man you are going to kill? Additionally, if Devon was paid to do this by someone, he must not have been paid very much—only one day later, he was trying to bum change off two women in a diner. Also, since Devon barely knew Shakespeare, would it be necessary for the killer, before killing Shakespeare, to hide his victim's face as Shakespeare's face was covered?

If Devon was not a hit man but still a killer, then what was his motive? He supposedly did not know John Shakespeare. If his motive was simply theft, then why didn't he take more from Shakespeare's home? Again, just days (even hours) after leaving Centralia, he seemed to be out of money.

Moreover, if Devon was in Centralia for only a day or so, we must also ask, When did he have the opportunity to kill John Shakespeare? From the time of their dinner at Pinky's until he left town, Devon seldom seemed to be out of the sight and the company of Bill Wham: first, at the restaurant, then back to Wham's residence and then the next morning in Wham's car on his way to Sandoval. If Devon was responsible for Shakespeare's murder, did he leave Centralia and then come back?

Also intriguing in the Quinn Devon saga was how quickly local authorities pivoted away from him as a suspect. By May 18, based mainly on a questionable local witness statement, which changed the possible death date for John Shakespeare, Devon was, according to police and a *Centralia Sentinel* headline, "Ruled Out as 'Trigger Man.'"[58]

Finally, there's an intriguing denouement, an imponderable, related to Devon's few short hours in Centralia. As mentioned, he was in Wham's office at one time and met Sheila Buxton, then one of Wham's employees. Devon took a shine to the eighteen-year-old and asked her to dinner. As noted, she turned him down. That made Devon free for dinner with Wham and John Shakespeare at Pinky's. But what if she had agreed? It is quite possible that Quinn Devon would never have crossed paths with John Shakespeare.

WILLIAM B. WHAM

It's also possible that had Bill Wham not come forward to tell police about Quinn Devon, neither the police nor anyone one else would ever have known anything about this mysterious hitchhiker.

It's doubtful that Curt Lackey would have gone to the police about him; Lackey didn't know that the paths of Devon and Shakespeare had even crossed. (In fact, Lackey was never interviewed by police about Devon.)[59]

But after John Shakespeare's murder became front-page news in Centralia on May 9, 1975, Wham contacted CPD's Chief Simon Franklin that same day with as much as he knew about Devon.[60]

Soon it became fact that, except for the individual or individuals who killed Shakespeare, William B. Wham was one of the last two people who ever saw Shake alive. That other person was Quinn Devon, who had, seemingly, vanished into thin air. Hence, Wham quickly became a key witness, giving the police insight into the last days, or possibly even the last hours, of John Shakespeare's life.

But besides being a key witness, Bill Wham also became, as least as far as the public seemed to be concerned, one of the murder's main suspects.

No one at the police department had to be told who Bill Wham or the Wham family was. Wham had been born in Centralia and was the town's most prominent attorney. He began his law studies at the University of Illinois only to have them interrupted by World War II. During his service, he was in the U.S. Navy. After the war, he resumed the pursuit of his law degree. He was admitted to the Illinois Bar in 1947. Soon after, he joined up with his grandfather's law firm, Wham & Wham, which was based in Centralia. He would go on to practice law in town for the next forty years.[61]

Lest we forget, hitchhiking was far more common in the 1970s than it is today. But even then, Wham's incredibly generous treatment of Quinn Devon, this man he had just met in Mt. Vernon, must have seemed at least a little bizarre. Wham not only gave him a ride but also brought him to his office and to dinner with John Shakespeare and then allowed the man to spend the night in his house, sleeping, we assume, just a few dozen feet from his teenage daughter's room.

But when Shubert Fox, a friend of Wham and Shakespeare, was spoken to by police about Wham's extreme generosity to the hitchhiker, Fox was not surprised, saying that it sounded typical of what he would do. As stated in the police report, "[I]f he thought some of them would enjoy the company of someone else, he would try to get the two people together." Further, Fox thought "nothing" of the fact that Wham brought a stranger to Shakespeare's residence[62] (a sentiment that was also shared by Wham's employee at the time Sheila Buxton).[63]

A popular, enduring theory today for the Shakespeare murder is that Wham—in a bizarre *Strangers on a Train*–type plot—wanted Shakespeare dead, and when he met Quinn Devon, he quickly talked Devon into doing the killing for him. But if it is extraordinarily strange that Wham picked up a hitchhiker, clothed him, took him to dinner, and then allowed him overnight into his home, then it is certainly even more outrageous to think that Wham could then turn this out-of-place Irishman so quickly and fully into a vicious killer.

Other parts of this theory don't quite add up either. What motive did Wham have for killing John Shakespeare? And how did Wham know he could trust Devon to do this and not run immediately to the police? If Devon was not a hitchhiker at all but just a man hired by Wham for this grisly crime, why make such a public display of Devon, "meeting" him in front of Curt Lackey, dining out with him and Shakespeare, and then bringing him home?

Also, when did this crime take place? If it was to be carried out, one would think that it would be when Shakespeare was dropped off at his house by Wham and Quinn, at about 9:00 p.m. on May 6. But when John Shakespeare's body was found, he was in his red running shorts. Certainly, Shakespeare did not wear those to dinner at Pinky's. If he was murdered that night after dinner, was he first given the chance to change clothes? If any combo of Wham and/or Devon was responsible for Shakespeare's death, did they drop Shakespeare off and then return? If that is true, how did they sneak out of Wham's home without ever being seen or heard by Wham's daughter or any neighbors? If Quinn acted alone, how then did he not only sneak out of Wham's home but also make his way to Shakespeare's home on a different side of town? The two homes are located nine-tenths of a mile away from each other, an estimated driving distance of three minutes, much longer if you were on foot.[64] (The Wham home is on Centralia's East Calumet Drive. In 1975, its house number was 15; it has since been renumbered.)[65]

As we'll see throughout the examination of the Shakespeare murder, there is still no known motive for this crime. And that goes for Bill Wham, too. Unless it was some personal vendetta, Wham did not seem to have anything to gain by killing John Shakespeare. Yes, Wham did eventually get named as executor of Shakespeare's estate (and granted, did draw a hefty fee for that for several years), but there is nothing to suggest that he knew that he would eventually be fulfilling that role. Besides, though he was not as wealthy as Shakespeare, Wham was a successful attorney already, certainly making more than enough already to ably support himself and his family.

As mentioned, on May 9, 1975, Wham alerted the police to his dinner with Shakespeare.[66] This information made it into the press. On May 13, 1975, Wham let it be known he would be answering no questions from reporters. Was Wham's sudden tight lip indicative of him knowing more than he was saying? Or was he just anxious to keep his name and the name of his family out of the local press? After all, being tied to an ongoing murder investigation is probably not a good advertisement for an attorney. It has long been speculated that Wham might have applied his local status and/or his wealth to various city entities—from the police to the press—to make sure he was embroiled as little as possible.

Regardless, two days later, he did tell a reporter that he didn't think Devon was involved in any way in the killing: "I don't think there's a Chinaman's chance that he did it. I think the police are on the wrong track."[67]

An enduring and prurient rumor about Bill Wham and the Shakespeare murder is that Wham was not only John's killer but also, at one time, his lover. Wham either murdered him after some sort of lovers' spat or killed him to prevent him for "outing" or blackmailing Wham within the community.

But there is no evidence that Wham was either gay or bisexual. He was married twice. His first wife, Mary Ann, passed away in 1974. He remarried—his second wife was Joan Behrens—in July 1976.[68] Further, if Wham was involved with Shakespeare in a sexual or romantic relationship and needed it to keep it secret, why be seen out and around town—for example, at Pinky's? Additionally, we have no evidence of Shakespeare being so vindictive as to attempt to "out" someone else. And besides, how would he do it and to what end? There was no Facebook or social media in 1975; how would Shakespeare have attempted to get the word out about Wham's personal life? Moreover, though he had lived there for twenty-five years, Shakespeare was still viewed as something of a newcomer and an eccentric one at that. Any attempt to taint Wham's public image would surely have just backfired on him and have little to no effect on Bill Wham.

Other questions persist in these various Wham/Shakespeare gay scenarios. John Shakespeare was certainly not the only gay man in Centralia at that time. If Wham was looking for a same-sex partner, why choose Shakespeare? Meanwhile, if Wham had other gay lovers throughout his life, why did he kill just this one and none of the others?

But perhaps the biggest outstanding issue regarding Bill Wham and the Shakespeare murder is why he was not more thoroughly interviewed by the police in 1975. Though he sat down with officers in November 1976 to discuss the case, there's no evidence of him being interrogated in 1975 other than a brief mention—one paragraph in the police files—of his dinner with Shakespeare and his meeting up with Quinn Devon earlier in the day. Was Wham not considered a suspect in 1975 and, hence, not interviewed? Or has a copy of his original interview somehow disappeared?

William B. Wham lived to be ninety-nine years old. He died in 2022.[69]

DAVID L. GADDY

In 1975, living just about a block and a half from Shakespeare's home was a nineteen-year-old man named David L. Gaddy.[70] Gaddy was a drug addict and already seemed to be quite well known to the police, press, and citizens of Centralia. In fact, in the first front-page article that the local newspaper published on the Shakespeare homicide, on the morning of May 9, 1975, Gaddy is the only possible suspect mentioned by name.[71] He was mentioned to reporters by Detective Simon Frankin, as Gaddy already had a warrant out for a Clinton County, Illinois gun offense, and he was known to own a .22.[72]

Gaddy was further implicated on May 15, when his neighbor David Goodin went to the police department and stated that he thought Gaddy might have been involved in the Shakespeare homicide.[73] Among the odder developments that Goodin pointed out concerning Gaddy was that he had just recently procured a brand-new Dodge van, though no one was quite sure where he got the money to buy it.[74]

Goodin further reported that on May 7, Gaddy came to his home and asked to borrow a gun. Goodin would not give Gaddy any of his own weapons, but Goodin had a gun in his possession that already belonged to Gaddy. Goodin returned that weapon to him. According to Goodin, he returned to Gaddy a .22 long rifle (serial number: 340570) with "4 or 5 boxes of shells." When Gaddy left Goodin's home on the evening of May 7, Goodin asked him what he was going to do with the gun. Gaddy replied he was "going to shoot someone."[75]

Goodin would not see Gaddy again until Monday, May 12, when Gaddy returned to Goodin's home. Once there, Gaddy supposedly started talking about the Shakespeare murder. Goodin said that he heard Shakespeare had been beaten; Gaddy replied that he had not heard that.[76] Based on this information, Centralia PD interviewed David Gaddy on May 14, 1975. Centralia police were also able to obtain a search warrant for his home. In the closet of Gaddy's home, they found a Winchester .22-caliber semiautomatic. A plastic bag containing five live cartridges was found along with the weapon and was confiscated.[77]

Later, this gun was test-fired by the IBI, but according to its report, "No positive identifications were made."[78]

That, apparently, closed the book on Gaddy as far as the CPD was concerned—at least, for the time being.

Not long after the Shakespeare killing, Gaddy moved out of Centralia and to Chula Vista, California. He joined the navy, but his naval career was short-lived; he was discharged from the military rather quickly to undergo a "psychological evaluation."[79]

After being forced out of the military, Gaddy found it hard to find employment. His wife, Mary Alice, whom he married in August 1982, worked to support the two of them.[80] She also endured his escalating drug problems, later stating that among the drugs her husband was using at that time were heroin, Seconal, and possibly even crystal meth.[81]

According to a couple of handwritten receipts found later, Gaddy did attempt to deal with some of his demons; he visited Chula Vista's South Bay Guidance Center several times.[82]

Then, in the early afternoon of September 28, 1982, David Gaddy walked into San Diego's Bay General Hospital. He attempted to admit himself, stating that he was coming off a drug binge and needed medication to alleviate his withdrawal pains. Hospital staff refused to give him any medication, but they were ready to admit him for a seventy-two-hour psych hold. Gaddy left the hospital but then returned fifteen minutes later, stating he had both a gun and a razor in his car and intended to kill himself if he were not administered a drug to ease his suffering.[83]

Staff managed to place Gaddy in an evaluation room and alert both hospital security and the police.[84]

When hospital security and police arrived on the scene, the already-agitated Gaddy became even more upset. Eventually, he reached into his rear pocket and pulled out a .25-caliber gun. Gaddy begged the police to kill him: "Shoot me, go ahead and shoot me!" Officers tried to talk him down and ordered him to drop his weapon. According to hospital records and news reports, Gaddy then "leveled" his gun at one of the officers and one was forced to fire. Gaddy died from a single gunshot wound.[85]

At the hospital, physicians attempted to save Gaddy's life but were unable to. David Gaddy was pronounced dead on September 28, 1982, at about 3:30 p.m.[86]

After Gaddy's death, Illinois investigators looked once more into him as possibly being John Shakespeare's killer.

Mary Alice Gaddy, David's widow, was first interviewed by the IBI in February 1983. She was asked about her late husband's possible ties to the Shakespeare murder. Mrs. Gaddy stated that, yes, she and her husband had, at least once, discussed the Shakespeare killing. She even once asked her late husband, point-blank, if he was the one who killed Shakespeare. Gaddy replied, "I wouldn't tell that to anyone."[87]

Gaddy had also once disclosed to his wife that he knew that Shakespeare had been bound and gagged. Later, officers asked Mrs. Gaddy if she thought her husband had killed John, but she did not think he did. She said, "He was too chicken. He was so much of a chicken that he wouldn't even commit suicide to himself, all he wanted to do was lay down and go to sleep," later adding, "He would make somebody shoot him."[88]

After speaking with Mrs. Gaddy, police also spoke to a man named Dennis Klinger, a neighbor and friend of Gaddy's in San Diego. Klinger related an odd story. It seems that just about a week before the hospital incident, Klinger, Gaddy and another male friend of theirs were sitting in Gaddy's apartment. Klinger noticed that the landlord had let his dogs out in the yard and made mention of it in passing. But Gaddy, strung out on drugs at the time, immediately panicked. Thinking Klinger had said "cops" and not "dogs," Gaddy ran to his closet and retrieved two guns, ready to barricade himself inside the house if necessary. Once Gaddy was calmed down, he told Klinger that he panicked because the cops were still after him for a seven-year-old murder that occurred in Centralia, Illinois.[89]

Despite this incident, Klinger concluded his interview with detectives by saying he believed his late friend was a "sweet guy" who could never kill anyone.[90]

At the time of the Shakespeare crime, Gaddy was living at 426½ South Sycamore Street in Centralia (about one block from Shakespeare's home). He lived there with a woman named Diana Norton—though supposedly they were just roommates and not romantically involved.[91]

In 1982, the courts subpoenaed Norton to see what she could still recall about Gaddy, specifically from around May 1975.[92]

In her interview, Norton explained that not long after her time living with Gaddy, she had suffered a "complete nervous breakdown" and was later subjected to various shock treatments. Though she could remember very little, she did recall that Gaddy did once own a small-caliber firearm that he had purchased through a mail-order company. She believed that was around May 1975.[93]

But authorities seemed to think she still might know more. Though Norton originally objected, she finally consented to be hypnotized to see if she could recall any other pertinent information. Five days after her initial interview, Norton returned to the police station and sat down with Fred Smith, a hypnotist and DCI agent.[94]

Norton was the only individual ever put under hypnosis during the course of the Shakespeare investigation.

With CPD Captain Jerry Edmondson and case agent James McCoy in the room, alongside Agent Smith, Norton was "put under" and answered various questions. Among her responses about those specific days: "David was acting weird….He was high on speed. Thought somebody was trying to shoot it out with him or something….I was scared. I couldn't control him."[95]

Under hypnosis, Norton (whose name is repeatedly mistyped in the report as "Horton") went on to state that Gaddy had two guns in his possession at the time, but she did not recall him owning any handcuffs. She did, however, mention one or two of his friends who he hung out with and who he often did drugs with.[96]

But these revelations from Norton didn't seem to move the Shakespeare investigation or the case against Gaddy forward.

Then, in 1983, still looking into the Shakespeare case, Centralia Detective Richard Simer and James McCoy went to the offices of the Centralia newspaper, the *Centralia Sentinel*. There they reviewed the classified ads for the months leading up to the Shakespeare murder. Was anyone at that time, they wondered, selling a .22 pistol? Eventually, they discovered several possible new leads for the source of the murder weapon. A man named Larry J. Walton sold a gun around then, as did a man named John Reynolds.[97] Most intriguing, however, was one sold by Keith Meredith in January 1975. It was an H&R .22 pistol with a six-inch barrel on it. The gun was sold for fifty-five dollars to another local man; Meredith could only remember the buyer had a last name starting with "G."[98]

Years later, after he was killed at the hospital, among the items found on Gaddy's person were his wallet (it contained one dollar and a variety of membership cards), a pair of sunglasses, a handgun and a pistol with an elongated barrel.[99]

MELVIN GAMBILL

Sometime during their investigation, the IBI was presented with a possible new suspect in the Shakespeare killing. His name was Melvin Gambill.

Though Gambill (frequently misspelled in police documents as "Gamble") held a bachelor's degree in social studies from Missouri State and had taught college in Murray, Kentucky, he was now living with his mother in Centralia. He told the police that he had been unemployed for over a year since losing his job teaching in the Odin, Illinois school system.[100]

Gambill was questioned by the IBI in October 1976. Gambill, it was believed, supposedly crossed paths with John Shakespeare when, some years prior, Gambill had expressed interest in starting a new Boy Scout troop in town or in joining the existing Explorer Scouts troop, the one Shakespeare was already mentoring alongside a local man named Ron Goff.[101]

Somehow Gambill's request for the latter was turned down. In their interview with Gambill, IBI officers then relayed to Gambill that they heard that it was John Shakespeare who had rejected him. But Gambill replied he had never heard that story and further denied that he had ever met Shakespeare.[102]

Further into this questioning, Gambill was asked if he owned any guns. He did. In fact, Gambill stated he had more than $3,500 invested in a variety of firearms, most of which he purchased from Mann's Gun Store in Pinckneyville, Illinois, or from Centralia's own Hansman Gun Shop.[103]

Gambill was also asked about his friends. He said they included Gary Carlson, who ran Fred and Mary's, a local tavern, and a man named Ron Closterman.[104]

Later on in the questioning, Gambill said he could not account for his whereabouts on May 7 or 8th of the previous year. He also refused to undergo a polygraph.[105]

But police never charged Gambill or seemed to pursue him further.

Interestingly, not long after his interview with the police, Gambill began getting in trouble with the authorities. Around 1977, he was convicted of attempted manslaughter in a shooting incident with area police. That resulted in a short prison stint.[106] By 1982, he was incarcerated again, this time in Salem, Illinois, after being charged with attempted murder and the unlawful use of a weapon. For that offense, Gambill had allegedly been in the backyard of Clifford Boles and threatened Boles and Boles's wife while brandishing a knife.[107] In April of '82, while Gambill was in jail in Decatur, Illinois, on that charge, a newspaper reported that he was on a prison hunger strike and had been for the past twenty-one days. He had just recently been moved to Salem Township Hospital and was being fed intravenously. State's Attorney Bob Matoush said of the situation, "I have no idea why he refuses to eat."[108]

How this matter resolved itself is not known. Gambill was living in Effingham when he died in 2014.[109]

DAVID W. HATLEY

As unbelievable as it might seem, the same week that Quinn Devon arrived in and departed Centralia and the same week that John Shakespeare was killed, another suspicious hitchhiker was in town and implicated himself in this murder. (In fact, there was even, among the police, a tenuous theory that these two hitchhikers met each other, perhaps in or around Sandoval, but that hypothesis dissipated early.)[110]

What is known is this: On May 10, 1975, a few days after the Shakespeare murder, an area man named Harry L. Wright contacted Centralia police to tell them of a hitchhiker he had picked up on May 5, near Sandoval, Illinois. According to Wright, he came upon the hitchhiker at about 9:35 a.m. just south of the B&O train tracks and not far from the city's Star Service Station. Wright dropped him off at Lee's Drug Store, located in downtown Centralia. According to Wright, he didn't see the man go into the store. Instead, the man went to an outdoor pay phone. Wright then drove away and never saw the young hitchhiker again.[111]

According to Wright's statement, the man's name was David Wayne Hatley; he was a white male, probably about six feet tall, about 130–35 pounds, with ear-length, light-colored hair. He was young and dressed ("poorly") in full-length trousers, possibly khaki in color, and had on what was later described as a jacket with "reddish sleeves."[112]

This sounds, of course, just like any other hitchhiker. But something else Wright told the police sparked their interest in this man. Wright said that, while driving into Centralia, Hatley asked specifically for directions to 514 South Pine Street. When Wright asked who he was looking for, Hatley said he didn't have a name, just an address. But that address was the home of John Shakespeare.[113]

Wright also said that, unlike most hitchhikers, Hatley carried nothing with him, no suitcase or backpack. In fact, the only thing Hatley had in his possession was a small box described by Wright as being about one foot long and "5 or 6 inches" around. It was wrapped in brown mailing paper.[114]

Though they were only together for about fifteen minutes in the car, Wright said that Hatley told him that he had just returned from visiting Las Vegas, via Iowa, on his motorcycle, a journey that supposedly took him a total of fifteen days.[115] (No one ever seemed to ask Hatley what happened to his motorcycle.)

Later, when Wright was asked by police if the man had a foreign accent, Wright said he did not.[116]

Unlike the mysterious Quinn Devon, more is known about David Wayne Hatley—though not too much. Hatley moved around a lot—Vegas, Florida, the Southwest—but he had some ties to southern Illinois. He was born in Murphysboro, a town about an hour's drive from Centralia, and had a cousin, Francis Minor, who lived in the Centralia area.[117]

Hatley seemed to have had a tough upbringing. His father, David Leroy Hartley, was arrested several times. In 1965, the elder Hatley was living in Grand Tower, Illinois, and arrested for failure to appear on a charge of forgery.[118] But around 1975, he was supposedly working, legitimately, as a full-time welder.[119]

Mostly, his son seemed to follow in his dad's early footsteps. In July 1974, a nineteen-year-old David Wayne Hatley was arrested in Clearwater, Florida, as part of a large burglary ring that stole and sold a variety of items but seemed to have a special interest in automobiles.[120] That same year, while residing in Sarasota, Hatley was also charged with forgery.[121]

After the tip from Wright, and unlike the Quinn Devon situation, investigators were able to track down, meet and interview David W. Hatley. It was easy to find Hatley, as he was in jail just down the road from Centralia in Salem, Illinois. A newspaper notice from May 28, 1975, reported that Hatley had just recently been charged with forgery (again) for attempting to cash two checks at a local Centralia bank.[122]

But whatever Hatley might have been in jail for at that time, Centralia Chief Franklin was far more interested in Shakespeare's murder than anything else the forger might have done.

As part of the interview with Hatley, Franklin learned that the phone call that Hatley placed outside Lee's Drug Store was supposedly a long-distance call to his mother.[123]

He also learned that, yes, Hatley did own a .22. He had purchased it from a local Centralia cab driver who—supposedly—found it in the back of his cab. In police records, the cab driver is identified as Terry Crane. Crane stated that he got the gun on May 4, 1975, when a passenger of his—George Shaw of Champaign, an IC railroad employee—found it in the back seat of the cab and handed it to him. Along with the gun, Crane also sold Hatley nine shells each wrapped in foil. According to Hatley, the gun in question was now at his parents' home in Cedar Lake, Indiana.[124] (How this gun came to be in Crane's backseat never seemed to be explored either.)

On June 2, 1975, James McCoy traveled to Cedar Lake and to the address (12921 Hilltop Drive) that Hatley provided them.[125] The elder Mr. Hatley was not at home, but David's stepmother, Mamie, was. McCoy, who was accompanied by Cedar Lake Officer Wesley N. Jenkins, confirmed with Mrs. Hatley that she did have a .22 (serial number 57544) in her possession. She retrieved the weapon, strongbox and all, and turned it over to them.[126]

The .22 was immediately sent to IBI headquarters. It was photographed and, in the lab, test-fired for a ballistic match. Unfortunately, according to an IBI letter from June 13, 1975, "no identifications were made" between this .22 and the one that killed John Shakespeare.[127] But if the gun test "cleared" Hatley to some degree, other factors about him were far harder to ignore. A *Centralia Sentinel* article, mainly on the hunt for Quinn Devon, made a brief, interesting mention of Hatley. It read, "[Hatley] had cashed some checks from the wife of a former partner in the Shakespeare Oil Co. It was first thought the checks might have been taken from Shakespeare's house, but this was never proven."[128] Then, in CPD notes on Hatley, there's a curious handwritten note that reads: "Find—5 checks in all—flushed three down toilet."[129]

Ultimately, some brief newspaper articles from this period fill in the details. Those checks were made out to Elizabeth McCarty, wife of Shakespeare Oil exec Jim McCarty; they were the ones Hatley forged and attempted to cash, earning him his most recent jail sentence.[130] What is not explained, however, is how he got his hands on these checks to begin with. Also, was it just coincidence that of all the uncashed checks Hatley could have somehow acquired, these were from Shakespeare's old namesake company?

In July 1975, Hatley was sentenced to nine months in prison for the forgeries.[131] But that same month, according to a newspaper article, Hatley was cleared by police as being responsible for the Shakespeare killing.[132]

Following his release from Salem's jail, Hatley continued his itinerant lifestyle, usually committing crimes along the way. His rap sheet is a steady string of offenses in several states and range from arrests for open container violations to trespassing to burglary.[133]

According to his brother, Hatley died of tuberculosis sometime in the early 2000s.[134]

So, did David Wayne Hatley kill John Shakespeare? Certainly the fact that he was seeking out Shakespeare's home address the very week that Shakespeare turned up dead is a stunning bit of information. And what were these checks from Shakespeare Oil?

But Hatley's possible involvement is hampered by the same old troubles: no real motive and nothing being stolen from Shakespeare's home.

If Hatley were a low-rent hit man sent by someone to kill Shakespeare, he was a pretty bottom-of-the-barrel assassin—unable to supply his own transportation or even knowing exactly where his would-be mark lived. Additionally, if someone paid Hatley to kill Shakespeare, he obviously wasn't paid very much, as he resumed his various other criminal enterprises quickly after the Shakespeare homicide.

Finally, there's a strange addendum to the Hatley inquiry. It has to do with the man who picked up Hatley and brought him to Centralia back in 1975. About ten years later, in June 1984, a man named Harry L. Wright with a listed age of fifty-seven was arrested on attempted murder charges stemming from the hold-up of the Star service station in Sandoval (ironically the same service station where he had dropped Hatley off at in 1975). After fleeing the scene, Wright sped down US 50 but was eventually apprehended after a high-speed chase and exchanging gunfire with officers.[135]

Assuming that these two Harry Wrights are the same person, how reliable of a witness was Wright to begin with? Could Wright just have known of Hatley and concocted this story, either to insert himself into this case or to frame Hatley? Did Wright and Hatley know each before this? (Hatley did have ties to the area.) Was there bad blood? Was this Wright's revenge? If it's the latter, that's a truly evil plan, pointing the finger right at someone and turning them into a suspect in a murder.

FRANK CIPELLE

Frank Cipelle's real name was Mathias Vincent Cipelle, and he was born in Michigan in 1930.[136] From early on in his life, it seems he liked cars and liked to drive them fast—sadly, sometimes with deadly consequences. In September 1950, in his native Detroit, twenty-year-old Cipelle sped through a red light at the city's intersection of Ten Mile and Little Mack, hitting another car and killing the father and son inside of it. Cipelle was arrested and charged with negligent homicide.[137] He was convicted of this crime, but the court gave him a choice of either going to jail or joining the military. He chose the latter and served in Korea.[138]

His time in the military did little to set him on the straight and narrow.

Still preoccupied with cars, when he returned to the States in 1954, he was arrested for violating the Dyer Act, an offense related to car theft. Convicted of that crime, Cipelle was given a five-year sentence but was then granted probation.[139] In 1959, however, he was arrested again for a probation violation and then again in 1960 on a fugitive warrant.[140] Then, in 1961 and 1962, he was arrested for the interstate transportation of stolen vehicles.[141]

In between all those illegal dealings, around 1957, Cipelle, also became a "business partner" with John Shakespeare in Shakespeare's Hoopeston,

Illinois–based car dealership.[142] But in November 1957, he was arrested for embezzling $100,000 from the operation.[143]

After his arrest, Cipelle was freed on a $5,000 bond.[144] Later, he was convicted of the crime.[145] Sometime after the Shakespeare murder, a friend of Shakespeare's conveyed to police just how angry Cipelle seemed to be at his sentencing.[146]

Not surprisingly, after Shakespeare's murder, Cipelle's long criminal record and his personal history with the victim piqued the interest of Illinois authorities, as did a report from someone (perhaps Ralph Porter) that Shakespeare was growing apprehensive about Cipelle coming back into his life.[147] Unfortunately, by this time, Cipelle was not an easy person to find, and the search for him extended well into late 1976.

Police and personnel from the IBI began their search in Champaign, Illinois, after being steered there by the town's city directory.[148]

In Champaign, the officers interviewed various previous business associates of Cipelle's, including one by the name of Hugo Gamboa who told them that Cipelle told him he was in John Shakespeare's will.[149] Meanwhile, the hotel manager at the local Regal 8 motel, where Cipelle had apparently recently stayed, directed them to a racetrack in Atlanta.[150]

Eventually, the search for Cipelle would take officers not only to Atlanta but also to Florida and Detroit. In Florida, Cipelle was rumored to have been employed by the Sebring Raceway. But a call by police to Sebring informed them that Cipelle had stopped working there sometime in 1975.[151]

Police followed just about every lead they could find to locate Cipelle. One of the tips they got was when a former associate of Cipelle's supposedly saw him on TV doing a commercial for Goodyear Tires.[152] Along the way, police allegedly unearthed various ties between Cipelle and organized crime.[153]

Finally, in November 1976, based on a forwarding phone number left at Sebring, they tracked Cipelle to Detroit, Michigan.[154] They even came upon a local Michigan phone number thought to be his. They phoned. The woman who answered the 313 area code number—later determined to be Cipelle's wife—answered as the business "Vehicle Testing." When police inquired further, the woman on the phone disclosed that this "business" was owned by Frank Cipelle.[155] If this phone call led police to Cipelle, it is not mentioned in their notes or reports.

While the police found that Cipelle was quite skillful at moving stealthily through the country, they found no other evidence to suggest he ever stepped foot in Centralia at any time in his life, let alone in or around May 1975. Further, when police asked Ralph Porter, Shakespeare's longtime handyman, if Shakespeare ever expressed any fear of Cipelle, Porter said, "Not at all."[156]

By the time John Shakespeare was murdered, it had been almost twenty years since Cipelle had been charged with embezzling from him. Could he have held a grudge that long? Further, if Cipelle believed he was in Shakespeare's will, that of course might be enough of a motive, but the bigger question is *why* would Frank Cipelle think that a man he once stole six figures from would leave him anything from his estate?

Meanwhile, in that same twenty-year interim, there's some suggestion that Cipelle might have belatedly righted himself and become a full law-abiding citizen. After 1959, there are no additional arrest records pertaining to him, and there's a handful of newspapers articles about him that seem to indicate that Cipelle was now on the up and up.[157]

Frank Cipelle died in December 2003.[158]

Bernard "Bernie" Gross

Every town has one or two (or more) local iconoclasts, even oddballs. Certainly, Centralia was no different. These neighbors are often strange and offbeat, but are they ever dangerous? After the murder of John Shakespeare, Centralia police began to wonder.

Specifically, they began to wonder about a local man named Bernard A. "Bernie" Gross. And they might have had every reason to wonder.

In 1975, Gross, though thirty-nine years old at this time, he was still living with his parents (who owned a local shop) in their home about six to seven blocks from the Shakespeare residence. That house was often referred to as the "Addams Family house," after the 1960s TV series, because of how spooky it seemed.

It was known around town that Gross was mentally "off." He often seemed paranoid, as he told anyone who would listen about the threat of mysterious "foreigners" coming into the country to take over the United States. Much to the consternation of the local newspaper staff, Gross often stopped by their offices to share with them his latest conspiracy theories.[159] He did the same—often on a daily basis—to the local fire department. There, he always warned anyone who would listen that they "were being watched."[160]

Though detectives—for some reason—did not get around to interviewing Gross about the Shakespeare murder until late 1976, they didn't have to work too hard to get him to chat. Apparently, Gross was quite anxious to sit down with investigators. When he did, Gross stated that he had known Shakespeare for "a number of years" and sometimes went over to his house to "shoot the bull." He added, however, that he had not been over in "quite some time."[161]

According to Shakespeare's handyman, Ralph Porter, when Gross would stop by (about "once a month"), Shakespeare, at first, seemed to humor Gross. Once, he even, again according to Porter, gave Gross an extra car body he had for him to "fix up." Shakespeare allegedly promised Bernie that once he was done with the body, he'd give Gross an engine to put in the car.[162] But it seems that with time, Gross started to outwear his welcome. According to Porter, he and Shakespeare discussed Gross on April 30, 1975.[163]

When Gross was finally interviewed by two IBI special agents, Gross's overall statement was described in police records as "rambling" and included a list of Centralia citizens who "could not be trusted."[164] Gross also indicated that he believed he was being followed.[165] In the interview, Gross refused to respond to many of the interviewers' questions, stating only that such information would "not be in the national interest."[166] Later, he asserted he did not kill John Shakespeare. When asked directly if he knew who had, Gross replied, "Not exactly."[167]

Despite law enforcement's instincts to dismiss Gross as a kook, various factors kept his name on the police's short list of suspects.

Gross stated that in the 1960s, he'd own a "white-handled" .22 but that the gun "didn't work" and that he had not seen the gun for a long period.[168] (Hence, Gross was unable to produce the weapon for forensic examination.) It was also said that Gross was known to frequently stop by a local service station every day to get himself a bottled soft drink. A bottle was later found in Shakespeare's home after Shakespeare was murdered.[169]

Then, the day that Shakespeare's body was found, Gross was among those at the scene. This was not that surprising, as many in the neighborhood did come out of their homes to see what the commotion was all about. However, Gross was accused of attempting to peek in the windows of the Shakespeare home before being shooed away by police.[170] Then, when Gross was later asked about how he first heard about Shakespeare, he said he'd heard it on the radio or television news.[171] But no station had yet reported the crime when Gross (and others) began to show up on Pine Street. Did Bernie mean police radio? And if so, where did he get that police radio?

Then, a local grocery store owner and friend of John Shakespeare's, Lee Hannon, informed area police that Shakespeare had recently become increasingly "leery" of Gross. Hannon also told police that Gross had come to the store just days after the murder to ask him what he thought about the killing, which Lee found to be an odd inquiry.[172] According to Hannon, Gross had at least one time before Shakespeare's death talked to him about buying a gun. Later, when asked, Hannon bluntly told the police that Gross was the one who "did it."[173]

Further, Ralph Porter, who was interviewed immediately after the murder, also straight-up accused Gross of the crime when he was asked by investigators about who might be responsible.[174] According to Porter—who, in time, would give two slightly different statements about Gross and the Shakespeare home—Gross had either once before somehow gained access to Shakespeare's basement or Porter once caught Gross attempting to access the basement.[175] In both scenarios, Porter chased Gross off. He also stated that Gross had recently been accusing Shakespeare of being a communist and that Shakespeare was growing increasingly fearful of what Gross might do to him.[176] Shake told Porter he was going to have to discourage Gross from coming around to the house. Porter also suggested that his boss change the locks.[177]

In 1976, and per what seemed to be standard operating procedure for the investigation, Gross took an IBI-administered polygraph test. He was asked, point-blank, such questions as "Did you shoot John Shakespeare in the head?" and "Did you put those handcuffs on John Shakespeare?" Gross answered "No" to all the questions posed to him. And Gross, seemingly, did not indicate deception in his answers, but in the end, polygraph examiner F.A. Paoletti invalidated the machine's findings due to the subject's "known emotional behavior."[178]

After that, nothing much else was heard of from Bernard Gross until about five years later. That's when, in late 1981, Gross's name entered the national news. In March of that year, President Reagan had almost been assassinated by John Hinckley. James Brady, Reagan's press secretary, was severely wounded in the attack. Brady hailed, originally, from Centralia. In fact, the Brady family lived just a few doors down the block from the Grosses.

Apparently, after Brady was shot, Gross became convinced that other current and former Centralia residents—especially from his block—were being marked for death. Gross acted on his suspicion and, four days after Brady was wounded, somehow made his way to Bethesda, Maryland, where Brady was being treated at Walter Reed Hospital. Then, somehow,

Bernie Gross, shabbily dressed and without any credentials, managed to gain access to Brady's private hospital room. Alerted by Brady's wife, the Secret Service quickly apprehended and handcuffed Gross and escorted him from the building.[179]

But that incident did little to dissuade Gross. Only days after, he made his way to the White House and onto a tour of the building. Once there, he splintered off from the rest of his group, only to be grabbed again by security and escorted out once more. On a later trip to D.C., Gross made his way to the White House again, this time requesting a meeting with First Lady Nancy Reagan. He was not successful and was again apprehended.[180]

Gross, who later married and moved to Las Vegas, died in 2023.[181]

Both Ralph Porter and Lee Hannon were convinced that Bernie Gross was the one who killed Shakespeare. Their firsthand accounts should count for something. Interesting then that local police did not find or question Gross until a full year after the murder. (Or if he was interviewed, that report has gone missing.)

Further, Gross's mental state might help explain away various oddities in this crime—for example, the odd, random items taken from the house.

But as weird as Bernie Gross might have been, he was never known to be violent, and make no mistake, Shakespeare's death was very much a violent crime. Still, past (and future) behavior is not always indicative; it can take just one thing or one day for someone to snap. Did Gross, who apparently thought Shakespeare was a bona fide communist, think he was doing the nation a favor by committing this crime? Gross would have, in some ways, been an easy person to pin this murder on, yet the CPD didn't. And there does not seem to be any reason for Gross to have been protected by any local powers that be.

RON GOFF

During the Shakespeare murder investigation, local educator Ron Goff was formally interviewed by the police (though not until October 1976), but he was never really considered a person of interest. However, revelations about him late in life brought a renewed scrutiny to this Centralian man.

When he spoke to the police, Goff stated he had been to Shakespeare's house "many times," and they have been described as "good friends." The main connection between him and John Shakespeare is that they were both troop leaders for the local Explorers Scouts.[182] As such, they saw each other weekly at the meetings of the troop, held on Wednesdays at the local Christian Church, and were almost always the two chaperones together on the camping and nature trips that the boys took to Missouri or even, once, to Canada.[183]

Police spoke to Goff early on, as he was able to provide some notable information regarding the last days of John Shakespeare's life.

As noted earlier, John Shakespeare was last seen alive (by Bill Wham and Quinn Devon) on the evening of Tuesday, May 6, 1975. But there was a scheduled weekly meeting of the Explorers set to take place on the evening of Wednesday, May 7.

At that time, the Explorers were only days away from going on a canoe trip down the Current River in Missouri. Shakespeare was to be one of the chaperones and was also underwriting the cost of the trip. It was assumed that he'd be at the meeting. Further, earlier in the week, two of the troop members, Pat Stedelin and Bob Magnan, ran into Shakespeare in town and reminded him of the upcoming Wednesday meeting. Shake seemed to indicate to the boys that he would be in attendance.[184]

On Wednesday night, however, Shakespeare didn't show. Thinking perhaps John had forgot, just before the start of the meeting Ron Goff asked one of the boys, said to be either Pat Stedelin or Bob Magnan, to head to the church's basement and call Shakespeare's home. But according to the police records, the Scout who was supposed to make the call later stated to police that he had forgotten to phone Shakespeare's house.[185]

Later, authorities would pronounce Thursday, May 8, as the day of John Shakespeare death.

But Goff's information reconfigures that timeline. Could Shakespeare have already been dead at least twenty-four hours before and that's why he didn't make the meeting? Additionally, Goff once mentioned that he himself stopped by the Shakespeare home on May 7. He tried the door to the house, but because it was locked, he walked away.[186] Does this mean that Goff had a habit of just walking up and letting himself in?

Ron Goff began working as a teacher in Irving, an elementary school, in Centralia in 1964.[187] Then, around 1980, Goff departed Centralia and its school system and moved to Edwardsville, Illinois, assuming the role of principal for Edwardsville Junior High. He held that position for ten years. He also remained active in local scouting. Then, in 1995, just after his retirement, Goff was charged with the aggravated sexual assault of an eleven-year-old boy, later identified in the press and court filings only as "J.L." The alleged incident occurred in 1990 at a church youth camp where Goff was volunteering as a camp counselor. Within days of the first charges being filed, other victims also came forth. Eventually, Goff would be charged with six counts of aggravated criminal sexual abuse, a Class 2 felony.[188]

In October 1995, Goff admitted to the abuse and was sentenced to five years in prison. Later, his teacher's pension was revoked, as it was determined that Goff was acting in his role as school principal when he groomed and abused the young boys. Goff eventually pleaded guilty to the charges, was ordered to jail and was also ordered onto the sex offenders registry.[189]

After serving his jail sentence, Goff moved to Ozark, Missouri. He died in April 2022.[190] Goff's later-in-life arrest cast him in a new light in terms of the Shakespeare murder. Though Goff was never charged with any abuse during his time in Centralia, it is questionable that he only began these practices later in life. Still, there remains no evidence of any abuse taking place in Centralia, and to date, no former Centralian students or Explorer Scouts have come forth with allegations against him.

But what if? What if Ron Goff abused a boy or boys around that time? If he had, could "good friend" John Shakespeare had found out something or suspected something of Goff? Did Shakespeare need to be silenced? But if so, if Shakespeare did know something, why didn't he immediately contact the police? It's also possible that John Shakespeare didn't know about Goff or any abuse but Goff thought he might, and that led to Shakespeare's murder.

The Goff revelations have also led to the "mistaken identity" theory of the Shakespeare murder. If there were rumors of a sexual predator active in local chapter of the Explorers, would people immediately have thought of Ron Goff? Goff was a married man and had two daughters at this time. Additionally, he worked in the local school system and was active in his church. Would he be the one everyone suspected? Or would suspicion more likely fall on the unmarried, eccentric man who most people around town knew of from his flashy cars and jogging down the streets in his red shorts?

THE SCOUT

If not Scout master Ron Goff, what about one of the Scouts themselves? Believe it or not, police also considered some of the former youthful troop members as perhaps the one(s) responsible for Shakespeare's death.

This suspicion might not be as far-fetched as it might seem. One of John's acquaintances once told police that he thought the Explorer boys "took advantage of him."[191]

The one Scout that the police seemed to show the most interest in was a seventeen-year-old at the time of the murder and had been counted among the onlookers outside of Shakespeare's house on the night the body was discovered.[192]

The boy was also, on the evening of May 8, at the about-to-start Explorers meeting at the church, the one where Shakespeare was expected but never showed. Ron Goff later told police that he had told one of the boys to call Shakespeare's home and see if he was coming to the meeting that night.[193] But when questioned, the Scout implied that he was the one who was supposed to call but "forgot."[194] In a later statement to police, the Scout who was interviewed said "nobody at the meeting called" because Shakespeare "frequently missed Scout meetings."[195] Others were firm in stating that Shakespeare never missed these meetings.[196]

In his interview, conducted by police on September 30, 1976, and done only after he was Mirandized, the questioned Scout said he had been a member of the troop for about ten years. Along with going on group trips with Shakespeare, the Scout said he visited Shakespeare's house often, always at Shake's invitation and usually alongside other Scouts.[197]

In his interview, the young Scout said he had seen Shakespeare on the street a few days prior to his murder. He also said that he never saw any sort of handgun in Shakespeare's home.[198] Police asked him where he was on May 6, 7th, and 8th. The Scout stated he had spent each of those days with a friend of his who was also a onetime Scout member.[199]

Police also asked the Scout if he was aware of Shakespeare's habit of always locking his vehicles. The young man said that Shakespeare always did that. He also said he had also seen several motorcycles gathered at Shakespeare's home in the period just before the murder.[200]

Finally, the police notes of his interview show that the Scout also brought up the existence of three home movie–type films that Shakespeare had in his home.[201] Why this was brought up is not explained—neither was what is on these films. The three films in question, however, are still part of the collection of evidence at the Centralia police station. If they have ever been viewed, what is on those reels has never been made public.

The Scout would not be interviewed again. Additionally, attempts to interview him for this book went unacknowledged.

If any Centralia Scout, past or present, was involved with the Shakespeare murder, then they have certainly kept a powerful secret for a long time. But why would they do it? They would not, of course, be the first young person to do something ignorant, but something this wholly misguided? Why kill Shakespeare, a man all the troop members seemed to have liked? If they were looking for sudden riches, that's a possible motive, but then how were they going to explain their newfound wealth to their friends and their parents? If this was revenge, then we are still seeking the answer to revenge for what?

TONY "T.C." CUNNINGHAM

Like so many people profiled in these pages, in his youth, Tony "T.C." Cunningham was considered something of a ne'er-do-well. Even decades later, people on a Centralia message board still describe him as a "punk."[202]

To be fair, Cunningham had not had an easy life. He was raised a ward of the state, his life regulated by Illinois Children and Family Services.[203] Though his father, Don "Red" Cunningham, was still alive and, reportedly, living in the area, he had little to do with his son.[204] Tony also had a brother, Jeff Chambliss,[205] but Cunningham's only "family" it seems were his friends in a local "motorcycle club," alternately named the Night Riders or the Vendettas. Others in this Herrin, Illinois–based gang were Bill Ramsey, Delight Wooters, John McFarland, Mark Miller, Danny Richendollar, Bill Pergel, Richard Stull and Sherry Evans.[206]

In April 1975, not long before the Shakespeare murder, twenty-year-old Cunningham had just returned to Centralia after riding his motorcycle down to Daytona. He attended the races down there and was out of town for about ten days.[207] Once back in Illinois, on April 26, he contacted Richard Hines at Centralia's Personal Finance regarding a loan payment that was due on his motorcycle in May.[208] At the time, Cunningham didn't have the cash. To make the next payment, Cunningham told Hines he was hoping to borrow the money he needed—around $2,300—from his friend Sherry McCaskey.[209] Along with the loan payment, Cunningham also had to pay for the bike's insurance (about $40 a month), and he also owed money to a local garage for some recent repairs to the bike. In fact, the cycle was sitting in an area repair shop, and they would not release it until the bill had been paid.[210]

Then, a few days later, on May 16, Hines got another call from Cunningham. Cunningham told Hines that he now had the money.[211]

Cunningham's sudden windfall and his reputation around town soon attracted police attention. But what really landed him on the police's radar was that the fact that police soon discovered he one was of the few in town who had laid eyes on the mystery hitchhiker Quinn Devon.[212]

In a statement that Cunningham's seventeen-year-old friend Mark Miller gave to the police on May 11, Miller relayed how the two men met.[213]

Miller stated that on May 6, he was going to meet Cunningham for coffee at Centralia's Sheridan Café; they were to meet about 3:30 p.m. According to Miller, once the two got there, Tony saw some people he knew, and he went to talk to them. One of the people Miller observed at the restaurant was a man he described as six feet tall, redheaded, and about thirty-five years old. It was a man Miller said he had never seen before.[214]

Tony invited this man—later introduced as Quinn Devon—to sit with them. Miller would later describe Devon as "an outward and knowledgeable person." Miller continued, "He spoke with an accent and told me he was originally from Ireland." Miller described Devon's clothing as a light tan shirt (later described as similar to the torn fabric used to bind Shakespeare's feet) and closely matching pants and "white dock-type tennis shoes." Miller said Devon seemed anxious about finding work and was also a bit flirtatious with the various women inside the café and out on the street.[215]

Miller then stated that he, Cunningham, and Devon left the diner and walked to Bill Wham's office building in Centralia. Devon said that he had left his backpack at Wham's office and had to go retrieve it.[216]

Supposedly, at this time, while walking down the street, Devon offered the two other men a joint to smoke. Miller maintains that both he and Cunningham declined.[217]

When they arrived at the office, Cunningham and Miller waited outside while Devon went in. When Devon returned, he was wearing, again according to Miller, a "Levi jacket."[218]

On the way back to the diner, Cunningham and Devon began to discuss martial arts. Reportedly, Devon demonstrated his skills to Cunningham, including such feats as how he could "take a knife from my hand [using] only my bandana."[219]

At the time of the Shakespeare killing, Cunningham was living with a woman named Marilyn Ann Wilkinson. In a major ethics violation, Wilkinson, five years older than Tony, had been Cunningham's social worker while he was still a ward of the state.[220] Police interviewed Wilkinson on May 20. In her interview, she said that Tony did not own a small gun or a pair of handcuffs.[221]

Two days later, Wilkinson was given a polygraph by Centralia police. During the test, she was asked again if she knew anything about any handcuffs: "Did you see Tony Cunningham with a pair of handcuffs at your home on his belt?" "Have you seen a pair of handcuffs at your home in the last year?" Wilkinson answered "No" to both questions. But later, when her test results were reviewed, it was shown that Wilkinson failed some aspects of her lie detector test.[222]

Supposedly, Cunningham was worried about this. According to police records, he confided privately to Larry Yarborough, a local health food store employee, that he was worried about Marilyn speaking about the cuffs—because Cunningham did own a pair.[223]

Then, on June 10, 1975, Cunningham (who had always denied even knowing John Shakespeare) submitted to his own lie detector test administered by the police. A transcript of Cunningham's lie detector question-and-answer interview is still in evidence at the Centralia PD HQ. Interestingly, while they seemed to have asked Wilkinson about possession of a gun, Cunningham was, seemingly, not asked that question. Notably, no copy of a general police interrogation of Cunningham seems to exist.

During his lie detector session, Tony Cunningham was asked if he had been in the home of John Shakespeare when he was killed. He was asked if he had killed John Shakespeare. And he was asked if the handcuffs used in the crime belonged to him. He answered no to all questions. The administrator of the test, H. Dwight Whitlock, announced later that Cunningham had "passed" the test, showing no signs of deception.[224]

Cunningham's passing of the test did not, however, stop a relative of Cunningham's, Roy Cunningham (exact relation unknown), from coming forward and saying that he thought Tony was the one who killed Shakespeare.[225] Police also heard from a local confidential informant who said that Tony Cunningham had mentioned being in Shakespeare's home when Shakespeare was murdered. The informant also stated that Cunningham owned a pair of handcuffs.[226]

Though Cunningham seemed to have been cleared of this murder, he would continue to have a lot of violence in and around his life. Around the time of the Shakespeare murder, again according to police notes, he told several people that he thought his father was going to have him killed, but he never said why.[227] Meanwhile, another note in police files states that

Cunningham's old biker buddy Wayne Ramsey and he had just had a major falling out, and Ramsey said that he had a contract to kill Cunningham, though he did not mention the source of the contract.[228]

Was any of this for real?

For a certainty, about a year later, Cunningham was one of five people charged with robbing a man in Breese. Along with Cunningham, two of the other five were Mark Miller and Susan Casey.[229]

In between, however, Cunningham, with Miller, did seem to clean up his act for a time. He steered clear of lawbreaking long enough to open and run for several years Aiki Shin Tai Dojo, a local Centralia business that taught martial arts, mainly to young people. Their business opened on Broadway in Centralia, and later, after a fire took out most of that block, it reopened on Locust.[230]

But then, in 1994, Cunningham was arrested and convicted on a Class 2 felony of aggravated sexual abuse of an underage girl. Due to a plea bargain, he was given a four-year probation.[231] In 2016, the sixty-two-year-old Cunningham was arrested again on four counts of aggravated criminal sexual abuse. In 2017, assumedly waiting for the case to come to trial, Cunningham was arrested again for violating a protection order. On these latter counts, Cunningham eventually pleaded guilty and was sentenced to six years in prison.[232]

In 2022, Cunningham was serving his sentence in Clinton County when he was diagnosed with inoperable cancer. He was discharged from prison in 2022 on a compassionate release.[233] He died shortly thereafter.[234]

So, did Tony Cunningham kill John Shakespeare?

The irony of his meeting the major suspect Quinn Devon certainly does place him front and center among suspects. But could these two men have met and bonded and concocted this murderous plan so quickly?

Cunningham did, somehow, get the money that he needed for his motorcycle. Where did that come from? (One would think that during the summer months, a young man surrounded by so many farms could find various ways to earn some cash.)

When John Shakespeare's body was found, Shakespeare's wallet was empty—but would he have had on him upward of $2,000 in cash? Then, once Shakespeare was dead in the basement, why didn't Cunningham get greedy and grab other items from the house? Though fencing things from Shakespeare's home might have proved a challenge, one would think he'd at least take far more than what turned up missing from the home. We should also note that amid Cunningham's various crimes, either before or after the

Shakespeare murder, none were nearly as violent as what was inflicted on John Shakespeare.

When she was interviewed for this book, Cunningham's widow, Vanessa (who only met and married Tony well after the Shakespeare murder), recounted a story that her husband told her about those events of 1975. It is extraordinarily similar to Miller's account: met in the diner, walked down the street, that bandana trick. She also said that Cunningham went to the police of his own accord, and if that is true, it certainly seems to move TC down the list of probable suspects. If he was involved, why would he inform the police of his contact with the man who was, at that time, the lead person of interest in the case?[235]

Mrs. Cunningham also went on to say that her late husband eventually came to believe that the man he met that day in Centralia was a hit man sent to kill Shakespeare over some sort of business deal—perhaps, she thought, over some of Shakespeare's oil business interests.[236]

One odd detail of the Cunningham aspect of this case is that while police files contain copies of his lie detector results, there is no copy of a police interview. Did it get lost? Assuming, of course, it actually took place.

WILLIAM D. FLANIGAN

According to William D. Flanigan, who lived in Mt. Vernon at the time of John's death, he and Shakespeare had been friends for around fifteen years. The two bonded over their mutual love of cars. At one time, Flanigan supposedly even owned an Aston Martin. At some point, he was talking to Shake about buying John's 1953 Lancia.[237]

Along with cars, the two men often traveled over to Belleville, Illinois, together to attend auctions or car shows.[238] They also attended weekly (Wednesday and Thursday) language classes at the Berlitz School in Belleville, perhaps with Shakespeare eager to learn a new dialect for his upcoming extended stay in Europe. For their trips to the city, Flanigan would drive to Ashley, Illinois, and park the Jag he drove. Shakespeare would then pick him up and drive the two of them to the school in the city.[239]

Other times, according to Flanigan, he'd drive to Centralia just to visit John at his home. According to Flanigan's statement to police, he remembered being at the Pine Street house once when several teenagers were also there.[240]

Early in his life, Flanigan worked for the Illinois Central Railroad. Later, Flanigan lived and worked in St. Louis. In 1942–43, he worked at Curtiss-Wright (later McDonnell Douglas). According to his sister Ruth Gant, who was also interviewed by police, her brother suffered a nervous breakdown around that time and was later in the hospital at Farmington, Missouri. Later, he was transferred to a hospital in Anna, Illinois. After being discharged, he looked after their mother and father and then went to work for Air-Vac in St. Louis; he was with them from 1962 to 1963. Flanigan had an ex-wife and a son who were residing in Lincoln, Nebraska.[241]

Flanigan only really popped up on the police's radar because a car similar to one he drove was seen in and around Shakespeare's neighborhood quite close to the time of the murder.[242] Flanigan was interviewed about it by police in November 1976.[243]

Flanigan drove what was described as an "old green Jaguar." And a car of a similar description had been seen by two local boys—and Explorer Scouts—Bob Magnan and Pat Stedelin at various times around, or near, Shakespeare's home in the days and weeks before his murder.[244] Meanwhile, Shakespeare's neighbor Don Vonderhiede told police that he had seen *two* sportscars (one perhaps a Jag) parked in Shakespeare's driveway "on or about" May 7 or 8th.[245]

When interviewed by Centralia police and an IBI officer, Flanigan stated that on May 6–8, 1975, he was at home in Mt. Vernon and nowhere near Centralia. Flanigan further said that he had not been to Shakespeare's residence in at least the preceding thirty days.[246] Along with sightings of a car like his, police files state that Flanigan did finally change his story and admit that he had visited the Shakespeare home the Saturday prior to the murder. Flanigan, accompanied by a local man named Charles Draffen, stopped by the Pine Street address but spoke to Shakespeare only briefly, and Draffen remained in the car. Draffen later backed up Flanigan's story.[247]

This last visit might be the time that Flanigan was talking about when he told police that on his last visit to Shakespeare in Centralia, when he left, he was sure someone followed him as he drove off south toward I-64.[248]

When interviewed, Flanigan was not the most accommodating subject. First, he refused to tell the officers where he was currently employed.[249] (Though he was probably with the Mt. Vernon Car Company at this time, working in the engineering department.)[250] Then, according to the police report of the interaction, he refused to be photographed by them, as he did not want to be part of, as he called it, a "rogue's gallery." Then, when police asked if he would sit down for a polygraph test, Flanigan also declined. He claimed the results would be off as he suffered from high blood pressure and was also taking Dristan, as he had a cold. Later still, Flanigan advised the officers that their investigation should "start at a different level," a statement that he did not elaborate on.[251]

As was the norm for these Shakespeare-related interviews, the police asked Flanigan if he owned any firearms. He did, but only a large-bore hunting rifle. The police also asked if Shakespeare had ever "shown any affection for him or displayed any Homo-Sexual tendencies." Flanigan said no, he had not. Later, before the interview concluded, Flanigan stated that he believed John's oil holdings might have been the motive for him being killed. But again, he did not elaborate.[252]

If Flanigan was not at first considered a prime suspect in Shakespeare's murder, he certainly made himself one with his less than candid responses to various police questions and his resistance to the polygraph. But again, one is left with the issue, the question, of motive. What did this longtime friend of John's have to gain by killing him?

Still, CPD looked into Flanigan and even went so far as to speak to his brother-in-law Harley Quillman in Pinckneyville. Among the various lines of questioning that police inquired of Quillman was if Flanigan ever exhibited any "homosexual tendencies." Quillman said that "as far as he knew, he did not."[253]

Flanigan died in 1987.[254]

SAM ELLER

Like Flanigan, Sam Eller was a friend of John Shakespeare's. And like Flanigan, he, too, had an interest in acquiring Shakespeare's Lancia. In a handwritten note he sent to John, postmarked May 8, 1975, he said he wanted to buy the car and would be happy to send a deposit to secure the sale.[255]

For a time, Eller owned a motorcycle dealership in Danville, Indiana,[256] but at the time of the Shakespeare murder, he worked at Bullock Garages in Dayton, Ohio.[257] When he spoke to police on July 16, 1975, he said that his "permanent" home residence was on Rural Route 5 in Mt. Vernon, Illinois.[258]

In one of his interviews, Eller stated that he and Shakespeare had known each other for over twenty years and that he was once employed, in the

'50s, by John as a mechanic for Shakespeare's fleet of cars. Among the maintenance he did for the vehicles, Eller said he also refurbished various antique and used cars for John, and together, they had even raced them.[259]

Since various sports cars had allegedly been seen around the Shakespeare home near the time of the murder, the police were interested in what Eller drove. At that time, according to Eller, he was driving a 1966 Volkswagen.[260]

Eller offered to take a polygraph if the police wanted him to.[261] He also said he had no idea who would want his friend dead and that he had no knowledge of Shakespeare being homosexual but added that he never knew of any women he had ever dated.[262] He said John was a "very gentle" person who he had never known to be "violent or forceful."[263] At the conclusion of the interview, Eller stated that he'd be happy to help the investigation in any way he could.[264]

Though there was no record of hostility between Sam Eller and Shakespeare and the competition for buying the Lancia would seem too small of an issue to develop into such a brutal killing, authorities still tried to verify everything that Eller said. They reached out to Robert Snyder, Eller's boss in Dayton.[265] Snyder did talk about Eller's "frequently" taking off from the job, stating that he was often "going to go back home as he had some business to take care of."[266] Investigators also spoke with Duane Richards, a former employer of Eller's who said that Eller spoke often about a sports car of his that he owned up in Kankakee but that he believed it had been recently repossessed.[267] Later, it was also learned that Eller owned a shotgun and a couple of pistols.[268]

Specifically, around the time of the murder, May 7 or 8, 1975, Eller said he was at work in Dayton, something that seemed to be attested to by his letter to Shakespeare about the Lancia.

COLONEL E.C. HARWOOD

As mentioned in this book's earlier chapters "The Victim" and "The Estate," during the last few years of John Shakespeare's life, he actively invested in something called the Monte Sole project. It was (supposedly) being built in or near the city of Lugano, Switzerland. It was the creation of famed economist and friend of Shakespeare's Colonel E.C. Harwood.[269] Harwood's big plan was to create an almost utopian community that would,

Edward C. Harwood. *Authors' collection.*

among other things, be based on the gold standard. Eventually, Harwood even hoped to also open a university there.[270]

Though he was strongly cautioned by his business manager against putting his money toward this endeavor,[271] Shakespeare seemed to believe strongly in this proposed newfangled community. In fact, Shakespeare's upcoming multi-month sojourn to Switzerland was partly for him to check on his investment.

As noted, Shakespeare was only days away from seeing what—if anything—had been done in Switzerland.

Unfortunately, had he lived, he might have been in for a rude awakening. It seems almost nothing had been done in Switzerland, not with his money or anyone else's.

Strangely, when Shakespeare invested in the Monte Sole project, he signed a "Restricted Life Estate" document (which, assumedly, he read beforehand) that, unbelievably, named the Monte Sole project as the sole heir of Shakespeare's full financial investment when he died.[272] After Shakespeare's death, his family attempted to recoup, in full, his investment in Harwood's enterprise. It was not an easy task, as by that time, the bank financing it was in receivership. In the end, the family received only $150,000, a small fraction of what Shakespeare had put in.[273]

With Shakespeare's departure to Switzerland imminent, could someone connected to the project have panicked? What would have happened if Shakespeare discovered that his condo over there did not exist and almost nothing else did either? Further, with the unique clause in his original agreement, if Shakespeare died, he would not have seen the proposed community, and the community would be poised to inherit all of Shakespeare's fortune. Could that be a reason for murder?

OTHER SUSPECTS

Faced with a high-profile crime, CPD and the IBI were forced to cast their net wide in terms of their investigation. To make sure all their bases were covered, the Centralia police took a renewed look at various known local criminals they had previously encountered. They also had to turn their eye toward any and all criminals who might have similar MOs to the Shakespeare crime—for example, those who preyed on wealthy men or those who targeted gay men or those who used similar means in the robbing or killing of their victims.

Meanwhile, as soon as the Shakespeare murder hit the press, other police departments from around the state and even from other parts of the country reached out to Centralia officials to tell them of similar crimes in their area. Could there be, they wondered, a connection?

In the end, both CPD and the IBI felt they had no choice but to explore every avenue, every angle and every possible lead. After all, one of them might be the murderer of John Shakespeare.

Some of the individuals explored but eventually dismissed include those discussed in the following pages.

Jerry Sartain and George McKinney

As late as the early 1980s, via Illinois' Sangamon County, the Shakespeare investigation was alerted to two new possible suspects. Sangamon authorities even went so far as to send Centralia photos, bios and the prison records of these suspicious two.

Jerald Dee Sartain, age forty-seven at the time, and George Patrick McKinney, age fifty-six, were both incarcerated in Los Angeles for a triple homicide in which they subdued their victims with handcuffs and then killed them with a .22. Both men had ties to Illinois. Sartain had only recently been released from Marion (Illinois) Prison for a different crime, and McKinney was apprehended in Springfield, Illinois, before he was extradited to LA.[274]

The LA victims of the two men were husband-and-wife business owners Herbert and Virginia Charce, who were found dead in their residence. Delores Watson, an employee of the couple's business, was also killed. She was found dead four hours after the Charces, at a separate location.

These killings took place in October 1975.[275]

Before heading to California, could Sartain and McKinney have pulled a similar crime in Illinois, specifically in Centralia?

The Illinois police were at least a little suspicious of them, or at least of George McKinney. A weapon in his possession, a .22 with the serial number

WANTED BY THE FBI

FBI Identification Order No. 3660 and Wanted Flyer No. 318 on George Patrick Mc Kinney, with aliases, FBI No. 4,728,973 are hereby canceled as he was located near Ardmore, Oklahoma, on April 1, 1963. (4-2-63)

BANK ROBBERY ; ESCAPED FEDERAL PRISONER

GEORGE PATRICK MCKINNEY

Photographs taken 1959 FBI No. 4,728,973

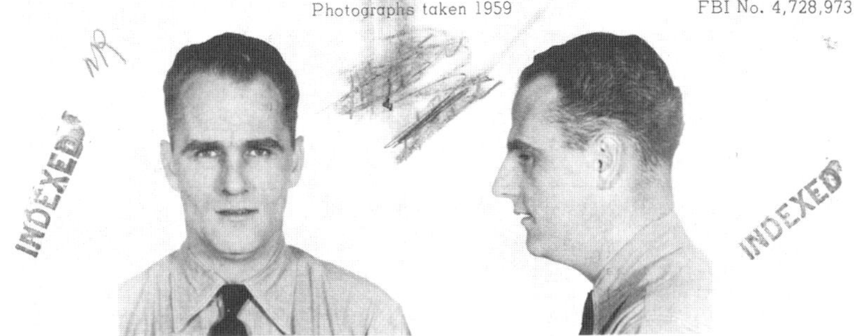

Aliases: Jack G. Beutel, Jackson George Beutel, Eric Fleming, Harold E. Fleming, Harold E. Fowler, Wade Patrick Johnson, R. A. Merlston, George W. Merrell, H. Mischkin, James Sincere, Levi Patrick Slamp, "Buddy" and others

DESCRIPTION

Age:	35, born May 17, 1927, Akron, Ohio		
Height:	5'11"	**Race:**	White
Weight:	165 pounds	**Nationality:**	American
Build:	Medium	**Occupations:**	Accountant, automobile salesman, bank clerk, cook, dental technician, dispatcher, hospital orderly, laborer, timekeeper
Hair:	Dark brown, curly, graying		
Eyes:	Blue		
Complexion:	Medium		

Scars and Marks: Pitted scar on forehead, vaccination scar left arm, pitted scar right elbow, small scar index finger left hand, cut scar base of left thumb, appendectomy scar; tattoos: two birds, scroll, heart, "Orian" on upper right arm.

Remarks: McKinney is reportedly proficient at golf and tennis.

Fingerprint Classification: 11 M 29 W MOO / I 32 W IOI 13

CRIMINAL RECORD

McKinney has been convicted of petty theft on a Government reservation, passing fictitious checks, and bank robbery and conspiracy.

CAUTION

MC KINNEY REPORTEDLY IS ARMED WITH THREE REVOLVERS, ONE OF WHICH IS CONCEALED IN WAISTBAND OF HIS TROUSERS. OTHER WEAPONS ARE USUALLY SECRETED NEAR HIM. CONSIDER ARMED AND EXTREMELY DANGEROUS.

A Federal warrant was issued March 7, 1963, at East St. Louis, Illinois, charging McKinney with bank robbery (Title 18, U. S. Code, Section 2113a). A Federal warrant was issued September 11, 1962, at Kansas City, Kansas, charging McKinney with escape from a Federal penitentiary in violation of Title 18, U. S. Code, Section 751.

IF YOU HAVE INFORMATION CONCERNING THIS PERSON, PLEASE NOTIFY ME OR CONTACT YOUR LOCAL FBI OFFICE. TELEPHONE NUMBER IS LISTED BELOW.

J. Edgar Hoover
DIRECTOR
FEDERAL BUREAU OF INVESTIGATION
UNITED STATES DEPARTMENT OF JUSTICE
WASHINGTON 25, D. C.
TELEPHONE, NATIONAL 8-7117

Wanted Flyer No. 318
March 13, 1963

A 1963 wanted poster for George McKinney. *Authors' collection.*

115991, was test-fired by the IBI in October 1976. But once again, no identification could be made.[276]

Robert Haag Jr.

Though he was the son Edwin Robert Haag Sr., an Illinois state representative, Robert Haag Jr. seemed to have a nose for trouble. In August 1962, when he was about twenty years old, Junior was charged with stealing a tractor from Affton, Missouri. Valued at $8,000, the tractor was later recovered off US Highway 50 near Carlyle, Illinois.[277]

After this incident, Haag Sr. obviously thought that his son needed some structure in his life. Since the senior Haag owned Haag Hatcheries in Breese, Illinois, he gave his son a job in the family business.

But despite his steady employment, Haag Jr. couldn't stay completely on the up and up. He gambled and was known to fraternize with various unsavory characters, some of whom had alleged ties to organized crime. They included William Sanders, Frank Crockett, and Malcolm Flynn.[278] (The latter two, notably, were also briefly considered in the Shakespeare killing.)

But police never got to interview Robert Haag Jr. He died by a self-inflicted gunshot wound on July 7, 1975. His body was found in the family home in a pool of blood at about four o'clock on the morning of the 7th. Haag had killed himself with his own personal firearm, a .38.[279] After his death, his body was transported to Moss Funeral Home in downtown Breese, and Haag was pronounced dead a few hours later.[280] But his death so soon after Shakespeare's death and his possible ties to various underworld figures made him a posthumous person of interest.

In fact, members of Haag's circle, family and friends were questioned about the Shakespeare murder and Haag's possible involvement only ten days after Haag's death.[281]

Detectives began their investigation into Haag by interviewing a local woman named Vernita Granda at her place of employment in Cahokia, Illinois.[282] Though Haag was married to a woman named Dorothy and had a daughter, Renee, Granada stated that she and the deceased had had a "close relationship for about the last eight weeks." Granada also related that Haag had, lately, been acting "very strangely," as he was being investigated by the IRS for both his business and personal taxes and was facing possible jail time due to various irregularities in his IRS filings. She further stated that he had seemed depressed and had trouble sleeping. But Granda said she knew of no dealings he ever had with "known hoodlums" (as they were described in the police report).[283]

About ten days after that interview, IBI agents spoke with Emil A. Garcia, president of the Haag Hatchery Inc. Though Garcia could not offer any "concrete" information on why Haag took his own life, he said he had noticed that Haag had been acting differently, not eating and barely speaking to customers or friends. Though Garcia stated that he had no great insight to Haag's finances, he had heard a rumor that Haag had recently lost $30,000 on a horse race. Later still, it was reported that Haag might have been in debt up to the tune of $200,000.[284] Investigators also spoke with Dorothy Haag, Haag's widow, who stated that she had no knowledge of any nefarious associates of her husband's.[285]

Authorities then waited two years before continuing their Haag inquiry. At that time, they went and interviewed a man named Enos McGee, a lifelong close friend of Haag's. McGee disclosed that though he now lived in Decatur, Illinois, he had lived in Centralia and was once a neighbor of John Shakespeare's. Further, McGee stated that Haag had visited Shakespeare's home at least once. Haag enjoyed collecting and trading coins and supposedly traveled often on behalf of his own collection and the collections of others.[286]

When asked by officers if he knew why Haag might have killed himself, McGee could find no reason, though he wondered if Haag feared possible jail time due to his tax troubles.[287]

At least that was one theory. Others speculated that it was more than just the power of the IRS that weighed heavily on Haag. It was reported that his depression seemed to only truly manifest itself in May 1975. Had he, faced with mounting debts and then being threatened by both the U.S. government and maybe even some of his less than savory associates, decided to do something desperate? Could he have traveled to Centralia—thirty-three miles from Breese—to the home of a well-known, wealthy man whom everyone knew lived alone and Haag knew owned valuable coins? And if he did, did he then feel guilty of something later on? Could he have felt guilty enough to finally take his own life?

Frank Crockett

Frank Crockett was primarily an arsonist, but in 1977, he was serving time in Illinois' Menard State Prison for burglary when he was interviewed by the

IBI about the Shakespeare murder. At the time he was interrogated, Crockett said that in the spring of 1975, he, with his accomplice Roy Lewis, had been hired—for $3,000—to burn down a three-story apartment building in Belleville, Illinois. Later that same year, for $500, he and Lewis had been hired to burn down a two-story home in East St. Louis, Illinois.[288]

Along with those and other arson crimes, Crockett also participated in various home invasions and burglaries, some of which occurred in Illinois. Working with two other accomplices, Roy Evans and Tom Whitt, the thieves particularly had an eye for valuable antiques, which they would then fence through a man named Ron Floyer.[289]

While he was interviewed by police, it's doubtful that Crockett was ever considered a serious suspect for the Shakespeare crime—but he did offer up a lot of interesting details about those he thought could be responsible. He mentioned his occasional partner, Lewis, who sometimes worked alongside two other men, Glen Chernich and Terry Wilson. The three of them once robbed two brothers who worked in the auto parts business. In that crime, they secured their victims with handcuffs.[290]

Then, when specifically asked about the Shakespeare killing, Crockett pointed the finger at fellow crooks Eddie Dunn and John Byrd as well as two men named Billy Johnston and Dougie Collegian. Crockett said that all four regularly preyed on homosexuals in the St. Louis area and that Dunn and Byrd had once robbed a gay man in Alton, Illinois.[291]

Cotrell Richardson

By 1975, Cotrell Richardson was well known to the Centralia cops and other area police. He had been getting into trouble with the law since at least 1964, when the then-thirty-five-year-old was arrested for a robbing a tavern.[292] He was in trouble again in January 1975 when he was arrested for punching a woman named Janet Sue Presberry in the face.[293] Five months later, in May 1975, he was indicted for intimidation to harm a woman named Edna Lee Davis if she didn't procure for him two bags of dog food.[294] That same month, he was charged with but pleaded not guilty to the delivery of cannabis.[295]

However, of greatest importance to Centralia police was Richardson's involvement in a home invasion and robbery that took place in Mt. Vernon in early 1975. Richardson and an accomplice, Leon McKinney, were suspected of robbing the home of Mt. Vernon Police Sergeant Lonnie

Odle and stealing, among other things, handcuffs and a gun. Later, however, when Centralia officers showed Odle photos of the handcuffs from the Shakespeare crime scene, he could not prove or disprove that they were his.[296]

When Odle did not definitively link the handcuffs from the Shakespeare murder to his handcuffs, Richardson was dropped as a viable suspect.

Randy S. Reyes

According to police files, as part of the investigation, CPD also looked at a man named Randy R. Reyes, a New Athens, Illinois carnival worker and thief who had been charged with burglary in July 1975. Seventeen years old at the time, he did not serve jail time but was put on probation.[297]

Hitchhiker No. 3

Stretching almost every law of believability, in May 1975, there was yet another hitchhiker who arrived in the Centralia area near the time of the Shakespeare homicide. Police briefly showed some interest in him. He had been picked up on May 4 by a seventeen-year-old local boy named Bill Stoafer. After Stoafer heard of the Shakespeare murder, he reported this hitchhiker to the police. According to Stoafer, he picked up the hitchhiker on Bell Club Road in Centralia. Stoafer later described that man as being about twenty-five years old and sporting a "bushy" beard. He said the man was on the heavier side, with blond, windblown hair. He was wearing jeans and carrying a small backpack. In the car, the hitchhiker said he was from Tucson, Arizona, and had a sister living in Central City, Illinois. The hitchhiker inquired about how to get to Elm Street, where his sister lived.[298]

Larry Luigs

In the CPD files, there is a fleeting note about Larry Luigs, a resident of Breese, Illinois, a neighboring town. In April 1970, thirty-one-year-old Luigs went to his place of employment, Breese Products, allegedly drunk, and then got into an argument and fought with some of his coworkers at the plant. Fired on the spot, Luigs then went into the plant's parking lot and cut up the convertible vinyl roof of one car and slashed the tires of another. He was arrested for that crime and later fined eighty-five dollars and ordered to pay restitution to the car owners.[299]

Five years later, on May 27, 1975, Luigs was indicted for rape in Centralia.[300] Two days after his indictment, he was interviewed by Centralia police about the Shakespeare case but was cleared in that inquiry.[301]

Roy Earl Schultz

Four days after finding Shakespeare's body, Illinois State Police looked into a man named Roy Earl Schultz. He had been apprehended for shooting a policeman in Kansas. Once caught, Schultz bragged of other crimes he committed. His choice of weapon was a .22.[302]

The Pirates

Perhaps one of the more intriguing—if tangential—theories/suspects in the Shakespeare case was a group of three young modern-day pirates.

In August 1971, at the Ala Wai Yacht Harbor in Waikiki, Hawaii, three men (Kerry D. Bryant, twenty-five; Michael R. Melton, twenty-four; and Mark E. Maynard, age twenty-seven) forcibly boarded the *Kamalii*, a seventy-five-foot ketch.[303] At gun and knifepoint, they forced the ship's three crewmen—Robert Waschkeit, John Freitas and Frank Power—to sail from the harbor with them aboard the yacht. Once at sea, the three hijackers subdued the three men by handcuffing their hands behind their backs, tying their ankles with rope and putting cotton over their mouths and then sealing them with surgical tape. One of them further stated to one of the hostages, "Make any noise and I'll kill you."[304]

Of the three thieves, Kerry Bryant became known to the three hostages as "The Slapper" for his frequent, open-handed hitting of the hostages. Though fellow pirate Michael Melton was a veteran of the Coast Guard, neither he nor his two cohorts seemed to know much about sailing or navigation. The three hostages hoped that their captors' incompetence would allow the three of them to be kept alive and on board.[305]

But they were wrong.

The day after seizing the yacht, about 120 miles south of Honolulu, Bryant and his fellow terrorists decided it was time to throw the crew members

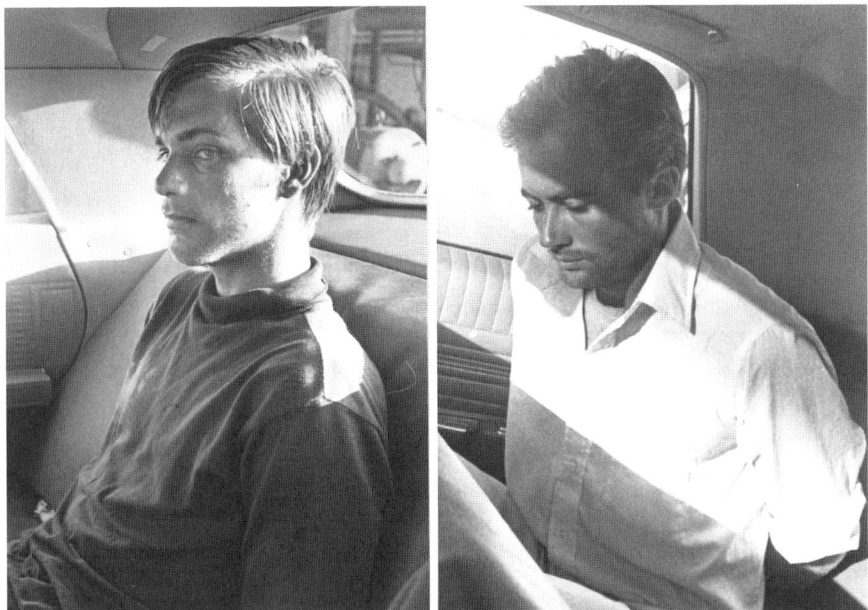

Would-be modern-day "pirates" Mark Maynard and Kerry Bryant after being apprehended. *Authors' collection.*

overboard. By that time, the vessel was in shark-infested waters, but the pirates made the men jump anyway. Then the pirates supposedly flipped a coin to decide if they should or shouldn't throw the boat's inflatable life raft overboard too. Maynard would later say to the men that they "got lucky."[306]

Once the three hostages were in the water, Maynard, Bryant and Melton deployed the ship's inflatable life raft. Then the *Kamalii* sped off.[307]

Apparently, the three hijackers held dreams of founding their own paradise—like modern-day Gauguins. But their fantasy didn't last long. Only days after their theft, the Coast Guard spotted the stolen boat and apprehended the three thieves.[308] Thankfully, a freighter on its way to Japan had developed engine problems, diverted from its usual course and came across the three former hostages, who were adrift in their life raft. After spending about five hours on the water, the men were rescued.[309]

After their arrest, the three young pirates each claimed not to be responsible for their crime due to "insanity." Their mental condition—exacerbated due to their heavy drug use—was later supported by a California psychiatrist who examined them.[310] Not long after their arrest and their diagnosis, the trio was sent to a mental hospital in Springfield, Missouri. After two months there, the three were judged "sane" and returned for trial. In the end, Maynard and Bryant were each sentenced to ten years in jail while Melton got probation.[311]

So, how does this all relate to Centralia and the murder of John Shakespeare? None of the trio of criminals had any known ties to Illinois. (Bryant and Melton were from California and Maynard was from Idaho.) But in January 1976, the editor of the *Centralia Sentinel*, John S. Wight, sent a letter to Mary Shakespeare, John Shakespeare's sister-in-law (his brother Henry's wife). In his letter, Wight asked her if, in conversations with John, he had ever mentioned any of the three hijackers and if she knew or recognized the name of E.L. Doneny, the owner of the stolen yacht.[312]

Though Mrs. Shakespeare replied, her letter seems to be lost. And Wight, interviewed recently, could not recall why he felt there was a connection between this odd, exotic, water-based Hawaiian crime and the Shakespeare killing, leaving this particular theory/inquiry just one of this mystery's many unanswered questions.[313]

OTHER LEADS

In March 1975, over in Collinsville, Illinois, a man named John A. Erickson reported to his local police a recent "homosexual contact" with a man he knew only as "Mike" that resulted in him being handcuffed and robbed. After first meeting, Erickson said he and Mike retreated to Erickson's home on Fairlane Avenue. Soon after, a friend of Mike's suddenly appeared at Erickson's home and forced himself into the residence. After being handcuffed—with police-grade handcuffs—and further subdued by a telephone cord pulled from the wall, the victim was threatened with an ice pick and told that he'd be stabbed by the pick "one half-inch for every dollar we find in this house."[314]

Luckily, the intruders never carried out their threat. After stealing sixty dollars in cash from the victim and various pieces of jewelry that belonged to the victim's mother, as well as some saving bonds and some silverware, the two men fled from the home.

Erickson was later able to free himself, but afraid to report the incident, he had his mother report the crime instead.[315]

It is not known if Erickson's assailants were ever caught.

In June 1975, police from Clayton, Missouri, alerted the Shakespeare investigation about the recent murder of a man named Fritz Whitehouse who had been killed along with his wife. Whitehouse, a wealthy man, traveled extensively and was known to be a collector of coins. Clayton cops wanted to inform Centralia since Whitehouse and his wife were tied up and shot and killed "several weeks" prior to the Shakespeare murder, supposedly when they admitted a person they did not know into their home.[316]

Also in June 1975, the IBI looked into a man named Don Rodes. (Some records spell his last name "Rhodes.") He was a forty-one-year-old out of Campbellsville, Kentucky, who had a misdemeanor record and owned a .22. For some reason, Kentucky State Police Captain Ralph Klein thought Rodes might be involved in the Shakespeare killing and phoned the IBI with Rodes's name and information. Centralia police later acquired Rodes's gun, which had been purchased from Gibsons Discount Store in Kentucky, and had it tested by the St. Louis office of the ATF. Evidently, it did not match, thus clearing Rodes of the crime.[317]

In May 1977, Robert A. Walkington, a detective in Jerseyville, Illinois (located about an hour and forty-five minutes north of Centralia), sent a letter to Centralia Police Chief Kermit Justice.[318] In the letter, Walkington related that in April 1975, he investigated the case of an elderly Jersey County man named Edward Zimmermann who had just been killed in a home invasion. Zimmerman lived alone and had been badly beaten, tied with electrical cords and eventually died from asphyxiation due to a gag being placed in his mouth. Interestingly, his home had not been ransacked, but the culprits did make off with $800 to $900 in U.S. currency that had been stored in the victim's safe. For this crime, three men—Francis L. Sheridan, David Fulks (possibly Faulks) and Robert Cash—were eventually apprehended and charged with murder and robbery.[319]

Walkington's letter to Centralia police noted that Cash was a redhead and spoke with a "deep noticeable accent." But the letter writer also noted that "Cash may have been in custody during the time of your homicide." When the letter was written, all three men were in jail at Menard, Illinois. Sheridan was serving a sentence of 70 to 210 years. Cash and Fulks obtained smaller sentences in exchange for their testimony against Sheridan.[320]

While the notion of this trio being responsible for Shakespeare's death is intriguing and maybe even plausible, certain factors work against it. For example, a gun was not involved in the Zimmermann killing, and unlike the Shakespeare home, something of some value was taken from the Zimmermann home. Further, if Cash and Fulks were happy to implicate Sheridan to obtain lesser prison sentences, then why not also divulge their (or his) role in the Centralia killing?

The Centralia police files on the Shakespeare murder also contained many names that the police must have considered but then dismissed as the probable killer(s). For example, there's a mention of David Hanley. Hanley was a local man who on May 6, 1975, boasted to someone that he soon "expected to get [his] hands on some money."[321] It seems that police never talked to him, but they did talk to his sister Lucy, who lived in the nearby town of Salem, Illinois. Interviewed on May 13, 1975, she said that her brother borrowed her car (a 1972 blue Maverick with a black top) with her permission around the time of the Shakespeare crime. But after borrowing the car, Hanley never returned it. In fact, Lucy had not seen him since that night. Police did promise to put an APB out on the vehicle.[322]

One day not long after the Shakespeare murder, the police of Elkville, Illinois—located about one hour from Centralia—called to inform Centralia investigators of a crime in their city that occurred in 1973. A man there was found dead in his garage, but it was unclear if he died from an accident or if it was a murder.[323]

According to Mike Justice, brother of Kermit Justice, though his sibling didn't always share too many details of any part of his work, Officer Justice thought that Shakespeare might have been murdered by a wholly different unmentioned transient. Centralia is a big railroad town with tracks that bisect the city. Those tracks were once regularly ridden by hoboes. According to Mike Justice, John Shakespeare often took extreme pity on these men of the rails and not only gave them money but also took a few back to his home to feed them. And—or so he heard—it was one of these vagabonds who, for whatever reason, probably killed John Shakespeare.[324]

The "hobo theory" is an intriguing one. It might explain if the Odin gun was the murder weapon how it got by the railroad tracks. But if that gun came from Pinckneyville, how did it end up in the hands of this random hobo? The hobo theory also makes the items taken from the Shakespeare residence seem even more odd: Why would a rider of the rails take a police scanner radio? Additionally, we must remember that Shakespeare, when his body was found, was clad only in his red running shorts. Would Shakespeare be "entertaining" in his home clad in such a manner? Also, how did the hobo get to Shakespeare's home if not driven there by Shakespeare in Shakespeare's car? And certainly, Shake was not driving around town in just his red running shorts.

Still, this theory is feasible, though no one else recalls Shakespeare taking a particular interest in the plight of the area hoboes.

Even onetime Centralia florist (and another local eccentric) Junior Patton had his name bandied about in terms of the Shakespeare mystery. A kind of hippie too, Patton had owned a local flower shop and was rumored to be gay. When his shop burned down, Patton never rebuilt and, in fact, never seemed to work again. He appeared to suffer more openly from mental illness, even briefly spending some time at a facility in Anna, Illinois. He often wandered the streets and was even known to dumpster dive for food or "recyclables." But this was done amid rabid rumors that Patton was actually quite wealthy, with most of his fortune stuffed in his mattress in the little shack that he called his home.[325]

As with Shakespeare, Patton was homosexual, and that seemed to be enough for some people to link him to John Shakespeare as well as his murder. But Patton and Shakespeare were never known to have interacted with each other, and further, for all of Patton's small-town eccentricity, he was never known to be cruel or violent.

Then there is the espionage accusation. During the war years, John Shakespeare did serve in intelligence while he was in the U.S. Navy. Later, in Centralia, he did reinforce his house with double locks and extra-control windows. And he did have a forest of antennas sprouting up from his lawn at one time. But during his life in Centralia and in the fifty years since his death, there has not been an ounce of evidence that ties Shakespeare to any super-secret government work and certainly nothing that would bring a foreign enemy to Centralia.

Alarmingly, the names shared here are probably not even the full list of people that local police and state authorities wondered about and looked into in relation to the death of John Shakespeare. During the first years of the Shakespeare inquiry, the CPD and the IBI looked into all sorts of angles as they might apply to this crime: organized crime, motorcycle gangs (with or without Tony Cunningham), and gambling operations that Shakespeare might have been involved with (he was not), among others.

In retrospect, William Flanigan was at least a little right in his desire not to be considered or added to this "rogue's gallery."

Still, for all this work, in the end, and to date, no one has ever been arrested for the Shakespeare homicide.

9
THE PRESS, THE CITY, AND THE RUMORS

In May 1975, the murder of John Shakespeare, "fishing heir," as he was usually described in printed pieces, was a big Midwestern—and beyond—news story.[1] The day after his body was discovered, not surprisingly, it was the front-page story in the local newspaper, the *Centralia Sentinel*.[2]

Under a headline that read, "Hands Handcuffed, Feet Bound: Shakespeare Found Dead," were essentially two stories. The first reported everything that was known about the crime at that time—where Shakespeare's body was found, who found it and the general appearance of the crime scene. This article, by John Wight, was also the press's first mention of William Wham dining with Shakespeare earlier in the week. It was also the first mention of mystery hitchhiker Quinn Devon as the third person at that meal.[3]

The other article on that newspaper's front page, starting just above the fold, was a biography of Shakespeare calling him a "man of unusual vitality."[4] It recounts Shakespeare's youth in Michigan, his move to Centralia in 1950 and his various business interests and hobbies. Strangely, this article also, for some reason, theorizes that Shakespeare was far less wealthy than many people might have thought.[5]

Photographs dot the page, too. There's a recent shot of Shakespeare, bearded and wearing glasses and attired in a sweater. There is a shot of the outside of Shakespeare's Pine Street home and a vintage photo of Shakespeare from the day he shipped off his Bugattis."[6]

Other photos reprinted were crime scene shots: a photo of Police Chief Simon Franklin looking over the blood-soaked basement concrete where Shakespeare's body had been lying; a shot of the same area from a different angle and without Franklin; and a shot of the body, covered and on a gurney, being removed via the side door of Shakespeare's home.[7]

While it is certainly understandable that Shakespeare's death dominated the Centralia headlines on May 9, 1975, the day after his body was discovered, what is peculiar is how little follow-up press coverage there seems to have been. Immediately after the crime, there were a handful of articles in the *Sentinel*, mainly pertaining to the hunt for Quinn Devon. Surprisingly, continued "daily coverage" of this crime story did not happen. Later in the month, there's mention of Shakespeare's memorial service and then a fleeting mention as part of a one-year anniversary article on the crime. But that's all.

Perhaps "true crime" coverage was not the thing then that it is now. Perhaps Centralians did not want a daily reminder that a brutal killer was quite possibly still living among them. Or perhaps since the only response that reporters seemed to get when they asked CPD about the latest on the case was "nothing new," eventually, the local press simply stopped asking.[8]

With no new facts coming out, gossip came along to fill in the blanks. Since that murder in May 1975, a profusion of rumors have circulated about why local news coverage was not more intensive. For example, could a wealthy, influential citizen in town have used his power on not only the police but also the press to keep his name and his family's name out of the headlines?

Adding weight to this possible part of the story is what *Sentinel* journalist Judith Joy discovered in 2015 when she went to write a story on the fortieth anniversary of the murder. When she went to the paper's archive for the Shakespeare file, it was completely gone.[9]

Today, we are left to speculate if the vanished file disappeared on purpose, if certain powers, inside or outside of the paper, made it go away.

THE RUMORS

The murder of John Shakespeare occurred at a difficult time for the Centralia Police Department. Just a year prior, it had faced a few internal and public relations controversies.[10] To investigate this and other police matters, in 1970 (five years before the Shakespeare homicide), the State of Illinois created the Vincennes Trail Law Enforcement Commission (VTLEC).[11]

The VTLEC was founded amid "speculation and accusations that various competing agencies were not sharing files and information."[12] The commission was further described as "a 12-county regions planning organization originated by the Illinois Law Enforcement Commission…concerned with the improvement of the Criminal Justice System within its area."[13]

After the Shakespeare murder, the commission, headed up at that point by Jack Sanders and Ronald Forehand, became involved in Centralia's investigation of the homicide.[14] It was a partnership that beget a plethora of issues, usually over issues of jurisdiction, availability of reports on the case and matters of just who was in charge of the overall investigation. Numerous letters, now among the evidence at the Centralia Police Department, document the terse—in fact, borderline hostile—interaction between the two organizations.[15]

For example, in August 1976, Kermit Justice wrote to Sanders and Forehand asking for updates on several outstanding Shakespeare case issues that the commission had, apparently, promised to look into. In the same letter, he demanded that "the Shakespeare case file [be] returned in full." He concluded the letter by writing, "I repeat again, I do not want the Major Case Squad working on any cases in the City of Centralia without full clearance through the office of the Chief of Police of Centralia."[16] (Which also begets the question of why the City of Centralia was so determined to remain in control of this investigation.)

A later supplementary report, this one from February 1977, details Jack Sanders and VTLEC's alleged failure to provide Centralia police with updates or to return much of the department's own paperwork.[17]

So whatever happened to these files? Were they ever returned to the CPD? Or are they still with the VTLEC? Repeated requests from the authors received no response.

Kermit Justice wrote his letter when he was the acting chief of police. He had obtained that role about two months prior, when long-serving Chief Simon Franklin was put on "voluntary" leave after he was accused, in June 1976, of two counts of shoplifting. Franklin was accused of stealing from

Centralia's Big John's supermarket a pack of cigarettes that cost $0.52 and, sometime later, $1.69 worth of cheese and Canadian bacon.[18]

Franklin maintained his innocence and, in the press, accused the arrest of being politically motived by various people in the city government wanting to end Centralia's city manager form of government.[19]

Inspired or affected by the Franklin charges or not, in March 1979, VTLEC's Jack Sanders then accused the entire Centralia Police Department of being "corrupt." Sanders alleged many of the officers were thieves and that others were being paid off by local taverns to disregard various criminal activities. Sanders would go on to accuse the department of misusing grant money and getting financial kickbacks from local contractors.[20] Sanders, who said at the time that the corruption dated back to 1974,[21] claimed that he had indisputable proof of all his accusations tucked away in a safe-deposit box.[22]

Eugene Qualls, Centralia's acting police chief by this time, responded to these accusations by saying he wanted to see proof.[23] But if Sanders ever revealed it, it is not documented anywhere. It should also be noted that at no time among his litany of corruption allegations against the CPD did Sanders ever reference the Shakespeare murder.

Nevertheless, in 1979, a grand jury was empaneled to investigate the alleged corruption of the Centralia force. While the inquiry might not have focused specifically on the John Shakespeare murder case, the case (though, again, it was possibly never mentioned by Sanders) seemed to have come as part of the probe. In the Shakespeare files at the CPD, there remains a small typed card. It is filed between two of the photos from the Shakespeare crime scene. The card is dated June 25, 1979. It reads, verbatim, in full:

> *Grand Jury Exhibit #1 – List of guns acquired by Eugene R. Qualls, Exhibit dated 6-18-79.*
>
> *Contents of Envelope – Grand Jury Exhibit #3. Gun File Centralia Police Department 74-75-76-77-78-79.*
>
> *Copy given to William Ludowski, S.A., A.T.F.*
> *Copy given to Ron Kincaid, S.A. F.B.I.*
> *Copy of Prints of Two Centralia Police Meeting with Jack Sanders. G.J. Exhibit No. 5.*
>
> *Copy of List of Donations Received From Centralia PD to Ron Kincaid 6/25/79*[24]

This short list presents a plethora of questions. For example, Item #1: Where did Qualls obtain all these guns? Could the Shakespeare murder weapon been among them? That same question seems to also pertain to Item #2. For Item #3, what "copy" is being discussed? For Item #4, are the "Prints" being noted here the two crime scene photos that were attached? Finally, Item #5, this "List of Donations" might reference the list of payoffs given to CPD members by area businesses.

In the end, Centralia's City Manager Bill Ramsey did order a thorough examination of the department.[25] Ultimately, one CPD officer was terminated for getting checks from a local tavern owner. In July 1979, a federal grand jury did not find any evidence of widespread misconduct or fraud in the CPD, and the case ended.[26] Afterward, CPD Chief Kermit Justice said, "The Department and myself have been totally vindicated."[27]

Similarly, Simon Franklin was later absolved of any wrongdoing when his accuser recanted his earlier testimony.[28] But overall, little seemed have changed.

In December 1979, Scott Pawlisa, age eighteen, and his brother Brian, seventeen, were shot by police after an attempted robbery of Centralia's Long John Silver's restaurant. The elder Pawlisa died not long after he was confronted by CPD as he attempted to escape the restaurant through its back door.[29] His brother ended up wounded and hospitalized but later died of his injuries.[30] Among the odder details of this crime was that as many as eight other youths knew of this crime in advance and parked in a lot opposite the restaurant the night of the hold-up to watch it unfold. Police supposedly had advance warning about the crime but didn't seem to work to prevent it.[31] Among the officers at the scene that night were Kermit Justice and Jerry Edmondson. After the death of the Pawlisa brothers, serious questions about police conduct were raised, and at least one civil suit against the force was filed by the boys' mother.[32]

Then, as if the police's internal and public image issues weren't enough, beginning in the early 1990s and continuing on for several years (and some say even up to today), various strange disappearances started occurring in a part Centralia known as the "Devil's Playground." Some of the vanishings: Joshua Mahaffey went missing in 1991 and has never been found; William Mark Bill Stutz was found dead in the area in 1997, and his killer is still at large; in 2011, Jared Hanna went missing and has never been found; and in 2014, James Romines went missing and has yet to be found.[33]

This ongoing unsolved series of either missing or murdered individuals has, as one can imagine, cast a long, disturbing, controversial pall over various institutions within the city of Centralia.

In 2016, Police Chief Doug Krutsinger resigned his post after it was reported he failed to or intentionally did not escalate to higher-level Illinois authorities an alleged murder-for-hire plot involving a local city councilman.[34]

Due to these unsolved crimes and all these accusations, the city's police force has had a far-from-stellar reputation both before and after the Shakespeare murder, thereby making accusations that they fumbled the investigation or purposely worked to hinder it rather easy (and popular) to believe.

But this then leads to a question: Could there be something so criminally askew within the highest ranks of the local force or perhaps even beyond it that has caused the killer(s) of John Shakespeare to never be held responsible? Beyond the police, are local judges and other office holders in on this as well? What about other organizations throughout the state? On various Facebook posts and other online discussions of the Shakespeare case, the phrase "cover-up" comes up with disturbing regularity.

Or is it possible that we all might just be a little too accustomed to movie and TV narratives where crimes are solved in usually an hour or, at least, under two? Hence, when a crime like the Shakespeare killing comes along and is not resolved in a speedy fashion, let alone in the past fifty years, is it then that we start to look for other, rather scandalous, reasons why?

When interviewed recently, former Centralia Police Chief Doug Krutsinger was philosophical about this still-unsolved crime from 1975. He said the Centralia squad "just didn't have the tools at the time."[35]

The lack of a solution does not, however, seem to be due to a lack of effort on the CPD's part. There are numerous police reports from late in 1976—a full year after John Shakespeare's death—that document that both the CPD and the IBI were still talking to witnesses, interrogating witnesses and running down leads (for example, all those .22s).

Then, even later than that, after David Gaddy (the former Centralian who died in California in a police shootout) died in 1982, officers traveled to California to interview Gaddy's widow and friends to see if he ever spoke about the Shakespeare murder.[36]

These efforts and the dates in which they occurred compel us to ask the question: If the solution to the Shakespeare murder is at the center of a major cover-up, why did these officers continue (or be allowed to continue) to put so much of the force's time and money into following up on these leads?

The cover-up theory is further harder to believe when you consider one of the stranger leads that the CPD later got and followed up on.

It began in April 2022, when a handwritten letter, originally sent to the Hoffman (IL) Police Department, was forwarded to Centralia police. It was from a Loral Richard "L.R." Huffman, a man then incarcerated in Romulus, New York, for a variety of offenses, including grand larceny.[37]

Huffman wrote in part:

> *Did you guys in this town have a guy named "Shakesper"* [sic] *murdered after being tied up, gagged and tortured and he gave up hidden-cash place? (Back of barn)*
>
> *If so, I met a* [sic] *old guy who was part of the 3 people that did it.*[38]

It appeared Mr. Huffman had become a prolific jailhouse snitch—apparently, one with a dependable reputation. Enclosed with his handwritten letter to the Centralia police were photocopies of three letters from various district attorneys attesting to Huffman's validity, veracity and helpfulness in previous cases by supplying "inside" information on several New York crimes.[39]

These letters eventually made their way to CPD Chief Steve Prather, who was deeply intrigued by the contents of Huffman's letter.

Prather wrote back quickly. In a letter dated May 3, 2002, he stated, "I would be very interested in speaking to you about your information."[40]

After that, the two men, located half a nation apart, had a prolific correspondence. The files of the CPD are thick with the back-and-forth of the two. They date from April 2002 to March 2003. Trying to reach each other, ideally, for a face-to-face meeting or even for a phone conversation, however, proved to be difficult. Huffman worried constantly about his personal safety should any of his fellow inmates discover he was planning to name names in this particular crime or others. Further, Huffman refused to disclose whatever he knew without a quid pro quo exchange. Before telling police what he knew, Huffman would go on to request a variety of things from a prison transfer to the removal of various disciplinary actions from his prison record to being added to a prison work-release program. At one point, he asked outright for cash ($500, to be exact).[41]

Prather, in his letters back to Huffman, repeatedly attempted to assuage Huffman's concerns about his safety, and should he provide useful information, Prather did promise to assist him any way he could. But Prather had no jurisdiction over Huffman's New York imprisonment and for Prather to convince New York officials to grant this prisoner any sort of leniency would take some major maneuvering.[42]

To his credit, Prather did not accept Huffman's assertions at face value and, in his correspondence, repeatedly asked for more and greater detail about the Shakespeare crime to make sure this was not all a ruse. And though much of the info that Huffman related in his letters had already been disclosed in the press, he was still quite convincing about what he might know. At one point, he even offered to draw a replica of the Shakespeare crime scene and send it to Prather.[43]

Finally, the Huffman-proffered information on the Shakespeare case came to a complete and abrupt end. In late 2003, New York's *Newsday* newspaper ran an extensive article titled "The Con Man" that exposed Huffman as a complete fraud. New York State Police Captain George Brown said, "Loral Huffman is a liar, and a thief, and that's about the nicest thing I can say about the guy." The article recounted how, throughout his incarceration, Huffman had been trading alleged "inside" information for various things, including an assortment of intrastate prison transfers. By the time this article appeared, Huffman's completely made-up testimony had already tainted a number of New York–based cases.[44]

Now it seemed Huffman was expanding out to other jurisdictions all over the country. While the L.R. Huffman episode of the Shakespeare saga was a wild goose chase, it does evidence that, amid continuing community speculation of a local police cover-up—or even laziness or indifference—in the Shakespeare case, as late as the early 2000s, twenty-five years since the killing, Centralia police were still attempting to solve this infamous local crime.

Today, L.R. Huffman is no longer a "snitch," mainly because he's no longer in jail. He makes his home in Erie, Pennsylvania, and runs a "sentence negotiation" service. Calls and emails to him regarding the Shakespeare murder were not returned.

Even after the near debacle of the Huffman situation, the CPD did not give up on the Shakespeare case. In the decades since the Shakespeare killing, DNA testing capabilities have grown exponentially.

In 2013, much of the physical evidence from the case was sent to the Southern Illinois Forensic Science Center to be tested for DNA evidence.

Among the objects sent were the hair samples (including supposedly over two hundred pulled from the Wham residence) and the towels and the soda bottle found at the crime scene. But other than determining that the hairs were human and Caucasian in nature, little else was learned from the hair samples, and the only blood found on the towels belonged to Shakespeare. As for all the other items, they proved to have been so mishandled or overhandled over the years that it was impossible to obtain any useful information.[45]

Not to be deterred, when new Centralia Police Chief Doug Krutsinger took over the department in 2014, he resubmitted all the Shakespeare evidence again for DNA testing, including a few stray brown hairs found at the crime scene. Sadly, this second attempt was no more successful than the previous one.[46]

Oddly, when Krutsinger arrived for his first day at his new job, he found all the Shakespeare-related reports, files and even its physical evidence, loose and unorganized, in some open boxes shoved in the corner of his new office. He eventually acquired an agent from the Springfield office to come and organize it all.[47]

Despite all this activity—which seems substantial for a case that is half a century old—public opinion about the force's mishandling of the investigation is prevalent. There are even persistent rumors (so far unsubstantiated) that, over the years, producers of various "cold case"– and "unsolved mystery"–type TV programs have approached both the CPD and Centralia's city government wanting to do one of their episodes on the Shakespeare crime but have always been denied.

Does the Centralia PD not want that sort of scrutiny? Are they, as has been suggested, embarrassed by this open case? Or do they just not want the kind of attention that could recast their small Midwestern city as some sort of "Murder-ville," the way that the lovely bayside community of Amityville, New York, has seen itself irrevocably reinvented as horror central?

Another popular thought surrounding the Shakespeare situation is a lingering accusation lodged at the local police that maintains the CPD has, over the years, purposely "lost" or destroyed evidence. But in evidence at the CPD today is everything from the towels that once hid Shakespeare's face to the yellow electrical cord, the handcuffs and the gag that was stuffed in his mouth—even two potential murder weapons are still all in the possession of the Centralia PD. Furthermore, a voluminous collection of reports, statements, photographs, polygraph tests results, correspondence and personal ephemera is there as well.

There's a rumor that even one or two of the suspected firearms associated with the case have been lost or even sold at auction (though guns are not normally ever a part of police auctions).[48]

Still, some peculiar items are missing—like the soda bottle, the paperback book, and the comic book said to have been found at the crime scene.

When Shakespeare friend and later suspect in his killing William Flanigan was interviewed again by police in October 1976, he said that "about one and a half weeks ago," he had attended an auction where some of Shakespeare's file cabinets were up for sale. Alarmingly, he said that within those cabinets were copies of canceled checks, correspondence and other personal papers. These documents might have contained illuminating statements and information. Were these items reviewed by the police before the cabinets were sold?[49]

And it does seem extremely odd that among all the police records and reports currently at the Centralia station, interview reports with Bill Wham (assuming one was made in 1975) as well as documentation pertaining to interviews with Bernie Gross and Tony Cunningham are all missing. Of all the things that could go missing, why reports regarding these three men? (It is possible that Wham was never viewed as a suspect and, therefore, may never have been formerly interviewed by the police.)

Other irregularities abound. For example, why were none of the staff of Pinky's spoken to—as far as we know—to try to learn more about Quinn Devon?

All that said, for any sort of major cover-up to have occurred is one thing, but could it have endured all this time? For fifty years and through various different police personnel and city administrations? And just who is still being protected all this time later? And what is in place that could still be shielding them from being exposed? Who, among those who might still be alive, still has that kind of power and influence to make sure that the truth remains hidden?

The local police department rumors about the murder of John Shakespeare are not the only thick and prevalent theories. Around town there are members of the community who hold a "syndicate" of organized crime responsible for the murder. There are those suspicious of Shakespeare's family.

Unfounded rumors tied to Shakespeare's alleged pedophilia are rampant too. One rumor says that Shakespeare was too close to a local underage boy and, as some sort of amends after his death, left him one of his sports cars in his will. But this is not true: Shakespeare died intestate, and his car collection was later sold at auction with its proceeds divided among his heirs.

Sometime in the 2010s, on the now defunct website Topix.com, a John Shakespeare Murder/Centralia interactive blog was created. It endured for years and eventually clocked in over one thousand threads and sub-threads. But, being the internet, it allowed for an untold number of messages (many of them posted anonymously) that were impossible to verify, not to mention often hard to believe. Did Junior Patton once trespass at St. Mary's Hospital in Centralia? Is this a tell-tale sign of a deeper psychology of his? Was Shakespeare once the victim of a "gay bashing" in New Orleans? Did Shakespeare sometimes make films—and of what nature—during Explorer trips? Not long after the murder, longtime Centralia physician Dr. John Stedelin—whose son had been an Explorer Scout in Shakespeare's troop—suffered a major breakdown and was forced to close his practice for many months. He, in the parlance of the town, "went to Anna," Anna being a nearby town and the location of the area's nearest mental health facility. What was the genesis of his mental health crisis? Could it be guilt or the knowing of something he wished he didn't? When she was working on her podcast about the crime, Ashley Casseday said she was approached by someone with "ties" to the CPD and they told her that the police knew who did it but that person was dead, and it's impossible to prosecute the dead. That's certainly an intriguing statement; at the time she was told this, prominent figures in the case—like Wham, Cunningham and Goff—were all still living.[50]

Theories as to "whodunit" and why abounded too. Along with discussion of all the usual aforementioned suspects, there was a theory that Shakespeare was involved in some sort of consensual sexual relationship with another local and also closeted man that, obviously, ended abruptly and horribly.

Was there some sort of neighborhood beef—over what, no one knows—that somehow escalated to this deadly outcome?

Equal parts intriguing and salacious, all these various accusations and suppositions manage to have one thing in common—no supporting evidence whatsoever.

CONCLUSION

So, who killed John Shakespeare?

Even with the combined efforts of so many people over the years, including the Centralia Police Department and the Illinois Bureau of Investigation, we don't seem to be any closer to definitively answering that question today than anyone was back in 1975.

Perhaps the question we should ask now is, "Will we ever solve this?"

While it is perhaps possible that some new clue will be unearthed that breaks the case open, the better bet is that some newfangled technological advancement—something we might not even be able to conceive of yet—might eventually create new tools to identify the culprit or culprits behind this crime.

We must also face the fact that all of this case's speculation of political cover-ups, serial killers, sex crimes, angry ex–business associates, hitchhikers, hired hit men, and latter-day pirates have just been so much (reckless) folly. There remains a possibility that this murder was the result of a regular, garden-variety home invasion/robbery that just went horribly, completely awry and resulted in the death of John W. Shakespeare.

Of course, if it were a robber, or robbers, someone is still responsible for ending the life of this vital, generous, and well-liked man who, even at an age usually defined as "elderly," still seemed to have a lot he wanted to do and to give to the world.

The grave marker for John Shakespeare, Kalamazoo, Michigan. *Authors' collection.*

We can only hope that no matter how long it takes, what police officer Kermit Justice said in 1977 will eventually prove to be correct: "We'll get the guy someday."

EPILOGUE

Finally, among all the police reports and the boxes of physical evidence related to the Shakespeare murder that are stored at the Centralia Police Station, there is this letter. It is typed, double-spaced and two pages long. It is dated May 14, 1975. It was sent to Simon Franklin and is from a longtime friend of John Shakespeare's, a man named Dr. Floyd E. Boys. Dr. Boys was then living in Charlottesville, Virginia. He wrote:

Dear Mr. Simon:

When our engineer friend from the Cleveland area telephoned us this morning and reported the sad news about the violent death of my old friend, John Shakespeare of Centralia, we were very upset. I am sending this note to thank you for the kindness and courtesy of phoning us late this afternoon (Eastern time), and giving us a brief report regarding the tragic affair—your call being made in reply to an earlier in the day telephone inquiry by my wife when I was out of the apartment.

John and I grew up together in Kalamazoo, Michigan, went to the same schools, knew each others' parents, and have kept in touch with each other over the years. Since he never married, and led a rather lonely existence, I am glad to say that our home in Urbana, Illinois (I lived there from 1949 to 1965) was frequently visited by John, and he became a great favorite of our two daughters. In recent years, he became acquainted with our six grand-children, and was equally well loved and admired by the grand-children as by their parents and grand-parents.

I trust that you can eventually find the culprit, and that you can see to it that he never is released into society for the remainder of the man's life....

John and I were older than his brother, Henry, and, although I have met Henry in years gone by, I really don't know him at all. I am glad that you were able to locate Henry, and that he, in turn, could attend personally to the last attentions for his brother. It will be appreciated if you will give Henry my address, and if you will kindly ask him to write me a note where, we in turn, can write him to express our sorrow at this tragic event.

If I can ever do anything for John's case, or for your police force or for you personally, do not hesitate to let me know.

Thanking you kindly for your thoughtfulness in telephoning us, and with thanks for your attentions to John's case, I remain

Very sincerely yours,

Floyd E. Boys [signature]

NOTES

1. The Victim

1. Interview with Mark Stedelin, May 20, 2024.
2. "John William Shakespeare (1905–1975)," Find a Grave, https://www.findagrave.com.
3. "John William Shakespeare (1905–1975)."
4. Judith Joy, "40 Years After His Death, John Shakespeare's Murder Remains an Unsolved Mystery," *Centralia Sentinel*, December 6, 2015.
5. "John William Shakespeare (1905–1975)."
6. E-mail correspondence with Eric Jeska, August 2, 2024.
7. Tom Cotter, "The Robber Baron's Bugatti Boondoggle," *Barn Finds*, June 2, 2013, https://barnfinds.com.
8. Cotter, "Robber Baron's Bugatti."
9. Douglas Steward, "The History of the Shakespeare Company" (master's thesis, Kalamazoo College, undated), kzoo.edu.
10. Steward, "History of the Shakespeare Company."
11. "About Us," Shakespeare Marine, shakespeare-marine.com.
12. "John William Shakespeare (1905–1975)."
13. Cotter, "Robber Baron's Bugatti."
14. Interview with Eric Jeska, August 6, 2024.
15. "Boiling Pot Ad Drive Assure's Book's Success," *Kalamazoo College Index*, January 1, 1924.
16. "Bock Made Head of Chemistry Club," *Kalamazoo College Index*, January 1, 1928.

17. Don Sherman, "A Used-Car Deal for the Ages: 30 Bugattis Sold for a Song," *New York Times*, May 23, 2010, https://www.nytimes.com.
18. E. Jeska, interview.
19. E. Jeska, interview.
20. Jack Rice, "Murder Within the Walls of Privacy," *St. Louis Post-Dispatch*, June 15, 1975.
21. "Obituary: John Shakespeare," *Centralia Sentinel*, May 11, 1975.
22. Joy, "40 Years After His Death."
23. Joy, "40 Years After His Death."
24. Joy, "40 Years After His Death."
25. John Wight, "Shakespeare Found Murdered," *Centralia Sentinel*, May 9, 1975.
26. "Heads Salem Firm," *Evansville (IN) Press*, October 26, 1950.
27. "History," Shakespeare Aggregates, shakespeare-oil.com.
28. Joy, "40 Years After His Death."
29. Rice, "Murder Within the Walls."
30. Rice, "Murder Within the Walls."
31. Tour of 514 South Pine, Centralia, home, December 26, 2024.
32. Home tour.
33. Rice, "Murder Within the Walls."
34. Rice, "Murder Within the Walls."
35. Wight, "Shakespeare Found Murdered."
36. Wight, "Shakespeare Found Murdered."
37. Wight, "Shakespeare Found Murdered."
38. Joy, "40 Years After His Death."
39. Rich Simer, as told to Jay Borum, *Diary of a Detective: Small Town…Big Secrets* (Independently published, 2017).
40. Stedelin, interview.
41. Joy, "40 Years After His Death."
42. Stedelin, interview.
43. These items are in evidence at the Centralia Illinois Police Department.
44. "Collector Gets Fabulous Auto," *Chicago Tribune*, September 7, 1956.
45. "Collector Gets Fabulous Auto."
46. "Collector Gets Fabulous Auto."
47. "Collector Gets Fabulous Auto."
48. "Sports Car," *News-Democrat* (Belleville, IL), June 16, 1954.
49. Cotter, "Robber Baron's Bugatti."
50. Joy, "40 Years After His Death."
51. "Shakespeare (Of Centralia) Helps Driver of Ferrari," *Herald and Review* (Decatur, IL), November 21, 1954.

52. "All Results of John Shakespeare," Racing Sports Cars, https://www.racingsportscars.com/driver/results/John-Shakespeare-USA.html.
53. Wight, "Shakespeare Found Murdered."
54. John Shakespeare (USA) - Complete Archive - Racing Sports Cars.
55. Cotter, "Robber Baron's Bugatti."
56. E. Jeska, interview.
57. Interview with Dan Jeska, August 12, 2024.
58. Valerie Shakespeare, *It's an Artist's Life for Me!* (actual arts foundation, 2008).
59. Cotter, "Robber Baron's Bugatti."
60. Cotter, "Robber Baron's Bugatti."
61. Cotter, "Robber Baron's Bugatti."
62. Cotter, "Robber Baron's Bugatti."
63. Interview with Steve Duensing, April 8, 2024.
64. Jaap Horst, ed., "'Magnificent Bugs' Get Royal Treatment on Southern," *The Bugatti Revue* 11, no. 2, https://bugattirevue.com.
65. Horst, "'Magnificent Bugs' Get Royal Treatment."
66. Horst, "'Magnificent Bugs' Get Royal Treatment."
67. Eric Jeska, e-mail correspondence.
68. E. Jeska, e-mail correspondence.
69. E. Jeska, e-mail correspondence.
70. Joy, "40 Years After His Death."
71. Home tour.
72. Wight, "Shakespeare Found Murdered."
73. David Marshall, "Flouridation Controversy Hits Council," *Centralia Sentinel*, March 1, 1966.
74. Letter from John Shakespeare to Albert F. Gibson, undated.
75. Interview with Kirk Wilkins, May 2, 2024.
76. Wight, "Shakespeare Found Murdered."
77. E. Jeska, interview.
78. "Rotarian Election Edwin Stanford; Hear CTHS Chorus," *Centralia Sentinel*, March 28, 1955.
79. "Rotarians See Film on Fishing," *Centralia Sentinel*, May 23, 1955.
80. "Planning Down Under Excursion," *Centralia Sentinel*, April 11, 1973.
81. "Australia Slides Shown to Lions," *Centralia Sentinel*, June 24, 1973.
82. "Ready to Roll," *Centralia Sentinel*, October 31, 1955.
83. Wight, "Shakespeare Found Murdered."
84. Wight, "Shakespeare Found Murdered."
85. Home tour.
86. Home tour.

87. Home tour.
88. Duensing, interview.
89. Interview with Craig Hensley, September 13, 2024.
90. Hensley, interview.
91. Interview with Kirby Dipert, June 6, 2024.
92. Stedelin, interview.
93. Wight, "Shakespeare Found Murdered."
94. Wight, "Shakespeare Found Murdered."
95. Letter from Mary McCallum to John Shakespeare, February 13, 1974.
96. Handwritten police notes, CPD, May 15, 1975.
97. Ashley Casseday and Stephen Garland, hosts, *Keep It Weird*, podcast, "Murder in the Midwest," 2018, https://www.keepitweirdpodcast.com.
98. Simer, *Diary of a Detective*, 98.
99. Letter from John Shakespeare to unknown person, undated, c. 1975.
100. Handwritten police notes (William Flanigan), CPD, January 23, 1976.
101. Letter from John Shakespeare to RobinsonBank, Ltd., January 28, 1975.
102. Information about John Shakespeare's assets at the time of his death were gleaned, mainly, from his correspondence to and from his onetime financial consultant Albert F. Gibson. These include letters dated November 10, 1973; January 15, 1974; and June 27, 1974.
103. Katy Delay, *Gold and Freedom: A Biographical Sketch of Edward C. Harwood* (CreateSpace, 2013).
104. Wight, "Shakespeare Found Murdered."
105. Letter from Albert F. Gibson to John Shakespeare, January 15, 1974.
106. Letter from John Shakespeare to Albert F. Gibson, November 10, 1973.
107. Raymond Craib, "The Brief Life and Watery Death of a '70s Libertarian Micronation," *Slate*, May 21, 2022.
108. Rice, "Murder Within the Walls."
109. Joy, "40 Years After His Death."
110. "Kenneth H. Cooper, MD, MPH," Cooper Aerobics, https://www.cooperaerobics.com.
111. Letter from John Shakespeare to unknown person, undated, c. 1975.
112. Interview with Tim Loughran, April 12, 2024.
113. Letter from John Shakespeare to unknown person, undated, c. 1975.

2. The Crime

1. "Assistance to Police Dept., Illinois," IBI complaint memorandum, May 13, 1975.
2. "Assistance to Police Dept."
3. Letter from R.L. Austin, Crime Scene Technician, to Simon Franklin, CPD, May 13, 1975.
4. "Detail Page," CPD, undated.
5. "Voluntary Statement: Ralph Porter," CPD, May 9, 1975.
6. "Ralph Porter."
7. "Ralph Porter."
8. "Detail Page," CPD, undated.
9. "To Report Interview with Pathologist Cesar Gallego, M.D.," IBI investigative memorandum, May 14, 1975.
10. "Detail Page," CPD, undated.
11. "Police Report No Motives in Centralia Man's Death," *Evansville (IN) Courier Press*, May 10, 1975.
12. Interview with Stanley Pokojski, January 22, 2025.
13. Austin, letter.
14. Austin, letter.
15. "To Report Interview with Ralph Mitchell Porter," IBI investigative memorandum, September 24, 1976.
16. Porter, IBI interview.
17. Handwritten police notes, CPD, October 8, 1976.
18. Austin, letter.
19. "Interview with Ralph Mitchell Porter."
20. Letter from C.L. McDougall, Crime Scene Technician, to Kermit Justice, CPD, February 8, 1977.
21. McDougall, letter.
22. Judith Joy, "40 Years After His Death, John Shakespeare's Murder Remains an Unsolved Mystery," *Centralia Sentinel*, December 6, 2015.

3. The Autopsy

1. Coroner's report: John W. Shakespeare, Marion County (Illinois), May 8, 1975.
2. Supplementary Report, Marion County, May 8, 1975.
3. John Wight, "Shakespeare Found Murdered," *Centralia Sentinel*, May 9, 1975.
4. Interview with Roger Campbell, June 12, 2024.
5. Campbell, interview.

6. St. Mary's Hospital: Autopsy Protocol: John W. Shakespeare (Centralia, IL), May 9, 1975.
7. "To Report Interview with Pathologist Cesar Gallego, MD," IBI investigative memorandum, May 14, 1975.
8. Campbell, interview.
9. Untitled typed report, credited to Edward E. Perry, May 8, 1975.
10. "Detail Page," Case #9-1-685, undated.
11. "Verdict of Coroner's Jury," State of Illinois, County of Marion, May 8, 1975.
12. Letter from R.L. Austin, IBI crime scene technician, to Simon Franklin, CPD, May 13, 1975.
13. Austin letter to Franklin.
14. Clinical summary: Post Mortem Findings: John Shakespeare; unaccredited, undated (hereafter Post Mortem Findings).
15. Chicago Toxicology Laboratory: Illinois Department of Public Health: John Shakespeare, May 12, 1975.
16. "Verdict of Coroner's Jury," State of Illinois, County of Marion, May 8, 1975.
17. Clinical summary: Post Mortem Findings.
18. Supplementary Report, Marion County, May 8, 1975.
19. Supplementary Report, May 8, 1975.
20. Gallego, IBI interview.
21. Gallego, IBI interview.
22. Gallego, IBI interview.
23. Gallego, IBI interview.
24. Gallego, IBI interview.
25. Gallego, IBI interview.
26. Postmortem findings.
27. X-Ray Report: Skull and Cervical Spine, R.J. Noveroske, MD, 400 South Pleasant Avenue, Centralia, IL, undated.
28. Office Memorandum from James McCoy to Richard Evans, Illinois Bureau of Investigation, November 8, 1975.
29. McCoy memorandum to Evans.
30. McCoy memorandum to Evans.
31. McCoy memorandum to Evans.
32. Rich Simer, as told to Jay Borum, *Diary of a Detective: Small Town...Big Secrets* (Independently published, 2017).
33. Untitled typed report, credited to Edward E. Perry, May 8, 1975.
34. Untitled report (Perry).
35. Untitled report (Perry).

4. The Timeline

1. Office Memorandum from James McCoy to Richard Evans, Illinois Bureau of Investigation, November 8, 1975.
2. John Wight, "Shakespeare Found Murdered," *Centralia Sentinel*, May 9, 1975.
3. Wight, "Shakespeare Found Murdered."
4. Ashley Casseday and Stephen Garland, hosts, *Keep It Weird*, podcast, "Murder in the Midwest," 2018, https://www.keepitweirdpodcast.com.
5. Wight, "Shakespeare Found Murdered."
6. "Voluntary Statement: Ralph Porter," CPD, May 9, 1975.
7. "To Report an Interview with Ralph Mitchell Porter," IBI investigative memorandum, September 24, 1976.
8. Porter, IBI interview.
9. Porter, IBI interview.
10. "Voluntary Statement: Ralph Porter."
11. Porter, IBI interview.
12. "Voluntary Statement: Ralph Porter."
13. "Voluntary Statement: Ralph Porter."
14. Porter, IBI interview.
15. Porter, IBI interview.
16. Porter, IBI interview.
17. "Voluntary Statement: Ralph Porter."
18. "Voluntary Statement: Ralph Porter."
19. "Voluntary Statement: Ralph Porter."
20. Dennis Montgomery, "Slaying of Wealthy, Colorful Man Unsolved After a Year," *Dixon (IL) Evening Telegraph*, May 11, 1976.
21. Handwritten police notes, CPD, September 21, 1976.
22. Handwritten police notes.
23. "To Report an Interview with Miss Ann Bingaman," IBI investigative memorandum, October 26, 1976.
24. Rich Simer, as told to Jay Borum, *Diary of a Detective: Small Town…Big Secrets* (Independently published, 2017).
25. John W. Shakespeare, Illinois Bell phone bill (618-532-9436), May 22, 1975.
26. Shakespeare phone bill.
27. Typed note from Centralia police files, undated.
28. "Shakespeare Murdered," *Dispatch* (Moline, IL), May 9, 1975.
29. Porter, IBI interview.
30. "To Report an Interview with Lyle Robert Leckrone," IBI investigative memorandum, October 12, 1976.
31. Leckrone, IBI interview.

5. The Estate

1. Letter from John Shakespeare to Albert F. Gibson, November 10, 1973.
2. Information about John Shakespeare's assets at the time of his death were gleaned, mainly, from his correspondence to and from his onetime financial consultant Albert F. Gibson. These include letters dated November 10, 1973; January 15, 1974; and June 27, 1974.
3. "In the Matter of the Estate of John W. Shakespeare, Deceased," Report of Sale of Personal Property, In the Circuit Court of Marion County, Illinois, June 20, 1977.
4. Ashley Casseday and Stephen Garland, hosts, *Keep It Weird*, podcast, "Murder in the Midwest," 2018, https://www.keepitweirdpodcast.com.
5. Interview with Theresa Greenwood, December 26, 2024.
6. Handwritten inventory from First National Bank, signed by Simon Franklin, Ralph Porter and others, undated.
7. Supplementary Report: Ralph Porter, May 8, 1975.
8. First National Bank, inventory.
9. "Centralian Was Man of Unusual Vitality," *Centralia Sentinel*, May 9, 1975.
10. "In the Matter of the Estate of John W. Shakespeare, Deceased," Current Report of Administration, Fourth Judicial Circuit Court, State of Illinois-Marion County, June 19, 1980.
11. "Shakespeare Murder Anniversary Tomorrow," *Centralia Sentinel*, May 7, 1976.
12. "Auction," *Mt. Vernon (IL) Register-News*, November 30, 1976.
13. "Exhibit C, Re: Estate of John Shakespeare," Ben J. Selkirk & Sons (St. Louis, MO), December 28, 1976.
14. "Exhibit C."
15. "Statement of Administrator, Estate of John W. Shakespeare, Deceased," undated.
16. "In the Matter of the Estate of John W. Shakespeare, Deceased," Petition Accompanying Administrator's Final Report, In the Circuit Court of Marion County, Illinois, June 19, 1980.
17. Letter from Schmoldt & Axmann to Meryl Rogers, First National Bank and Trust of Centralia, January 12, 1976.
18. Schmoldt & Axmann, letter.
19. John W. Shakespeare, Estate Tax Form (3614), IRS, May 1978.
20. John Shakespeare's heirs were Jean Krudener, Mary Alice Dies, Frank D. Shakespeare, Mary Jo Shakespeare Meyer, Henry Shakespeare, Marjorie A. Beresford, Valerie M. Shakespeare and William M. Shakespeare.
21. John W. Shakespeare, Estate Tax Form (3614).

6. The Revelation

1. All this evidence exists in three different boxes at the Centralia Police Force in Centralia, Illinois.
2. It should be noted that at the time of his death, some of John Shakespeare's friends vehemently denied that John was gay. In June 1975, his friend Harry Owens said to the *St. Louis Post-Dispatch*, "I traveled with John for years. I'd know, if anyone would. He liked women, he enjoyed their company…but he was at ease only with married women. Widows and young women…He said to me, 'I'd like to get married but I never know if she loved me or it was my money.'"
3. Cleo Kern, "Foreign Made Cars to Be Shown by Local Dealer at Hobby Show," *Indianapolis Star*, November 1, 1953.
4. "John Schaler III, Ex-Owner of Foreign-Auto Dealerships," *Indianapolis Star*, April 2, 2004.
5. "John Schaler III, Ex-Owner."
6. "Voluntary Statement," CPD, (John Schaler), undated.
7. "John Schaler III, Ex-Owner."
8. Supplementary Report: Homicide—John Shakespeare, Centralia Police Department, July 30, 1975.
9. "To Report Contact with the St. Louis Police Homicide Detectives in Regard to the Shakespeare Homicide," IBI investigative memorandum, November 11, 1976.
10. *Odyssey*, undated catalogue, circa 1975.
11. Canceled check #13678, First National Bank and Trust, Centralia, IL, John W. Shakespeare to Odyssey Club, April 24, 1975.
12. *Odyssey*.
13. *Odyssey*.
14. John W. Shakespeare, Illinois Bell phone bill (618-532-9436), May 22, 1975.
15. "To Report Interview with Pathologist Cesar Gallego, MD," IBI investigative memorandum, May 15, 1975.
16. "John Norman & The Delta Project: A Cover-Up of a Giant Trafficking Network and the Accomplice(s) of John Wayne Gacy," Reddit thread, https://www.reddit.com/r/conspiracytheories
17. "John Norman & The Delta Project."
18. Terry Sullivan and Peter T. Maiken, *Killer Clown: The John Wayne Gacy Murders* (Kensington, 2023).
19. "Gacy Tried to 'Protect' His Letter-Writing Friend," *Southern Illinoisan*, March 3, 1988.
20. "Obituary: Carolyn Terry," *Barre-Montpelier Times Argus*, May 6, 2006.

21. Lisa Marie Fuqua, "The Four on the Floor Wonderland Murders—True Crime," Medium, November 17, 2019, https://medium.com.
22. Fuqua, "Four on the Floor."
23. Fuqua, "Four on the Floor."
24. "John Norman & The Delta Project."
25. "John Norman & The Delta Project."
26. Fugua, "Four on the Floor."

7. The Investigation

1. "Final Chapter in Millionaire Shakespeare's Death Unwritten," *Southern Illinoisan* (Carbondale, IL), May 8, 1980.
2. Dennis Montgomery, "Slaying of Wealthy, Colorful Man Unsolved After a Year," *Dixon (IL) Evening Telegraph*, May 11, 1976.
3. "No Motive, Suspect Found in Man's Death," *Decatur (IL) Herald and Review*, July 9, 1975.
4. Charles Roberts, "Murder of Wealthy Centralia Man a Mystery—2 Years Later," *Mt. Vernon (IL) Register-News*, May 9, 1977.
5. "Detail Page," typed report from the CPD, undated.
6. IBI investigative memorandum, July 15, 1975.
7. Wight, "Shakespeare Found Murdered."
8. Supplementary Report, May 26, 1975.
9. Roberts, "Murder of Wealthy Centralia Man."
10. "To Report Contact with the St. Louis Police Homicide Detectives in Regard to the Shakespeare Homicide," IBI investigative memorandum, November 11, 1976.
11. "No Motive, Suspect Found."
12. Rich Simer, as told to Jay Borum, *Diary of a Detective: Small Town…Big Secrets* (Independently published, 2017).
13. "Voluntary Statement: Ralph Porter," CPD, May 9, 1975.
14. "Voluntary Statement: Ralph Porter."
15. "Voluntary Statement: Ralph Porter."
16. "Voluntary Statement: Ralph Porter."
17. "St. Louis, MO Weather History," Weather Underground, https://www.wunderground.com.
18. "Bound and Gagged in Basement," *Mt. Vernon (IL) Register-News*, May 9, 1975.
19. "Voluntary Statement: Ralph Porter."
20. Handwritten police notes (Ralph Porter), CPD, September 23, 1976.

21. "To Report Interview with Ralph Mitchell Porter," IBI investigative memorandum, September 24, 1976.
22. Porter, IBI interview.
23. Handwritten police notes (Ralph Porter), CPD, September 23, 1976.
24. Handwritten police notes (John Mays), CPD, May 10, 1975.
25. "To Report Interview with Robert Anthony Magnan," IBI investigative memorandum, October 12, 1976.
26. Handwritten police notes (Robert Magnan), CPD, undated.
27. Undated Magnan CPD notes.
28. Undated Magan CPD notes.
29. Undated Magan CPD notes.
30. Undated Magan CPD notes.
31. Undated Magan CPD notes.
32. Undated Magan CPD notes.
33. IBI investigative memorandum, January 1, 1983.
34. "John Shakespeare Homicide," report by the CRP, undated.
35. "To Report Information Received from Don Vonderhiede," IBI investigative memorandum, November 15, 1976.
36. "To Report Information Received from Mrs. Karen Meadur," IBI investigative memorandum, November 9, 1976.
37. Magnan, IBI interview.
38. Guestbook, Chapel of the Luer Funeral Home, John W. Shakespeare (Centralia, IL), May 11, 1975.
39. Guestbook, Riverside Cemetery (Kalamazoo, MI), May 12, 1975.
40. Letter from Roger C. Thompson, criminalist, to Simon Franklin, CPD, May 20, 1975.
41. Clinical summary: Post Mortem Findings: John Shakespeare; unaccredited, undated.
42. "To Report Interview with Max and Pearl Howell," IBI investigative memorandum, November 8, 1976.
43. "To Report Interview at Mann's Sporting Goods," IBI investigative memorandum, November 8, 1976.
44. Mann's Sporting Goods, IBI interview.
45. Typed noted from Officer Robert McGuire, undated.
46. "To Report Obtaining Custody of Hi-Standard 22 Pistol," IBI investigative memorandum, June 3, 1975.
47. "Information Obtained on High Standard 22 Magnum Pistol," IBI investigative memorandum, June 5, 1975.
48. Supplementary Report (#75-325), Hicks Trading Station, August 30, 1976.

49. IBI memorandum, January 1, 1983.
50. IBI memorandum, January 1, 1983.
51. Letter from Sam W. Nolen, deputy director, Department of Law Enforcement (Springfield, IL) to Special Agent James McCoy, February 24, 1983.
52. Newspaper clipping with Arland Speidel, unknown source, date.
53. Thompson letter to Franklin.
54. Letter from Timothy R. Dixon, criminalist, to Simon Franklin, CPD, May 21, 1975.
55. "Shakespeare Murder Anniversary Tomorrow," *Centralia Sentinel*, May 7, 1976.
56. Interview with Roger Campbell, June 12, 2024.
57. Handwritten police notes, CPD, September 30, 1976.
58. Letter from R.G. Jinks, Smith & Wesson, to Detective Richard L. Simer, CPD, December 1, 1976.
59. John Wight, "Shakespeare Found Murdered," *Centralia Sentinel*, May 9, 1975.
60. Wight, "Shakespeare Found Murdered."
61. "Shakespeare Murder Anniversary."
62. Letter from Glenn G. Schubert, forensic scientist, to Captain Rick Densmore, CPD, December 3, 2013.
63. Schubert letter to Densmore.
64. Schubert letter to Densmore.
65. Evidence holdings, Centralia Police Department (Centralia, IL).
66. "Final Chapter in Millionaire Shakespeare's Death."

8. The Suspects

1. John Wight, "Shakespeare Found Murdered," *Centralia Sentinel*, May 9, 1975.
2. Interview with Curt Lackey, May 13, 2024.
3. Lackey, interview.
4. Lackey, interview.
5. Lackey, interview.
6. Lackey, interview.
7. Lackey, interview.
8. "Interview with Attorney William Wham," IBI investigative memorandum, November 10, 1976.
9. Wham, IBI interview.
10. Wham, IBI interview.
11. "Voluntary Statement: Mark Miller," CPD, (May 11, 1975).
12. "Voluntary Statement: Mark Miller."

13. Wham, IBI interview.
14. "Voluntary Statement: Mark Miller."
15. "Voluntary Statement: Mark Miller."
16. Wham, IBI interview.
17. Wham, IBI interview.
18. Wham, IBI interview.
19. Wham, IBI interview.
20. "Shakespeare Murder Anniversary Tomorrow," *Centralia Sentinel*, May 7, 1976.
21. Wham, IBI interview.
22. Wham, IBI interview.
23. Wham, IBI interview.
24. Wham, IBI interview.
25. Wham, IBI interview.
26. Detail Page, Case #9-1-685, undated.
27. The police sketches from the four witnesses are among the evidence items at the Centralia Police Department.
28. Police sketches.
29. Interview with Janice Seiz, May 1, 2024.
30. "Memo from Mary Ann Carter," CPD, undated.
31. Interview with Sheila Buxton, May 2, 2024.
32. Buxton, interview.
33. Police sketches.
34. "Police Get Authority to Arrest Witness," *Decatur (IL) Herald*, May 15, 1975.
35. Handwritten police notes, CPD, May 14, 1975.
36. Police notes, May 14, 1975.
37. Police notes, May 14, 1975.
38. Police notes, May 14, 1975.
39. Police notes, May 14, 1975.
40. "Man Sought for Questioning in Centralia Murder Gets Away," *Mt. Vernon (IL) Register-News*, May 17, 1975.
41. "Crime Still Unsolved in Centralia," *Herald and Review* (Decatur, IL), May 8, 1977.
42. "Man Sought for Questioning in Centralia Murder."
43. "Crime Still Unsolved in Centralia."
44. "To Report the Records Check with the Memphis, Tennessee Police Department in Reference to Quinn Devon," IBI investigative memorandum, November 11, 1976.
45. "To Report the Investigation of Leads on Quinn Devon," IBI investigative memorandum, November 22, 1976.

46. Telex communication from Garda Siochana (Irish federal police), September 16, 1977.
47. Ashley Casseday and Stephen Garland, hosts, *Keep It Weird*, podcast, "Murder in the Midwest," 2018, https://www.keepitweirdpodcast.com.
48. "Irishman Ruled Out as 'Trigger Man,'" *Centralia Sunday Sentinel*, May 18, 1975.
49. "All Points Bulletin for Kidnapper," *Press-Tribune* (Roseville, CA), November 12, 1958.
50. Ann Rule, *But I Trusted You* (Gallery, 2021), 235+.
51. In the files of evidence at the Centralia Police Department is a typed list of aliases that Majors was known to have utilized in his crimes.
52. Rule, *But I Trusted You*.
53. Rule, *But I Trusted You*.
54. Rule, *But I Trusted You*.
55. Rule, *But I Trusted You*.
56. Casseday and Garland, "Murder in the Midwest."
57. U.S. Social Security Death Index, 1935–2014.
58. "Irishman Ruled Out as 'Trigger Man.'"
59. Lackey, interview.
60. "Detail Page" (William Wham), undated CPD notes, c. May 1975.
61. Bill Wham obituary, https://obituaries.morningsentinel.com.
62. "To Report Interview with Schubert D. Fox," IBI investigative memorandum, October 15, 1975.
63. Buxton, interview.
64. MapQuest directions between 514 South Pine Street and 15 East Calumet Street, https://www.mapquest.com.
65. Google Maps street view for 1000 South Lincoln Boulevard, https://www.google.com/maps.
66. "Detail Page," Case #9-1-685, undated.
67. John Wight, "Murder Investigation Is Believed 'At a Standstill,'" *Centralia Sentinel*, May 15, 1975.
68. Wham, obituary.
69. Wham, obituary.
70. "David Gaddy," IBI investigative memorandum, December 29, 1982.
71. Wight, "Murder Investigation."
72. Wight, "Murder Investigation."
73. "Voluntary Statement: D. Goodin," CPD, May 12, 1975.
74. "Voluntary Statement: D. Goodin."
75. "Voluntary Statement: D. Goodin."
76. "Voluntary Statement: D. Goodin."

77. "Constitutional Rights and Warnings (David Gaddy)," Centralia Police Department, May 14, 1975.
78. Letter from Roger C. Thompson, criminalist, IBI to Simon Franklin, CPD, May 20, 1975.
79. Supplemental report, Chula Vista (CA) Police Department, Mary Alice Gaddy, September 24, 1982.
80. M. Gaddy, supplemental report.
81. M. Gaddy, supplemental report.
82. A photocopy of a collection of membership cards, receipts and other ephemera of David Gaddy's can be found at the Centralia (IL) Police Department.
83. Richard T. Ruane, "Drug Addict Killed After Pulling Gun," *San Diego Union*, September 24, 1982.
84. Ruane, "Drug Addict Killed."
85. Letter from Marvin R. Brown, MD, ER physician (Bay General Community Hospital) to Detective Mark Croshier, Chula Vista (CA) Police Department, September 27, 1982.
86. Brown, letter to Croshier.
87. "To Report the Interview of Mary Alice Gaddy," IBI investigative memorandum, February 25, 1983.
88. M. Gaddy, supplemental report.
89. Supplemental report, Chula Vista (CA) Police Department, Dennis Klinger, undated.
90. Klinger, supplemental report.
91. IBI investigative report, Diana Horton, December 29, 1982.
92. Horton, IBI investigative report.
93. Horton, IBI investigative report.
94. IBI investigative report (hypnosis of Diana Norton, misspelled in records as Horton), January 1, 1983.
95. Horton, IBI hypnosis report.
96. Horton, IBI hypnosis report.
97. IBI investigative report, January 1, 1983.
98. "To Report Conversation with Keith Meredith," IBI investigative report, January 24, 1983.
99. Among the items pertaining to David Gaddy at the Centralia Police Department is a photocopy of a photo of the items Gaddy had on his person at the time of his death.
100. "To Report an Interview with Melvin Gambill," IBI investigative memorandum, November 11, 1976.

101. Gambill, IBI interview.
102. Gambill, IBI interview.
103. Gambill, IBI interview.
104. Gambill, IBI interview.
105. Gambill, IBI interview.
106. "Prisoner Continues Hunger Strike," *Herald and Review* (Decatur, IL), August 14, 1982.
107. "Prisoner Continues Hunger Strike."
108. "Prisoner Continues Hunger Strike."
109. "Melvin A. Gambill (1937–2014)," Find a Grave Memorial, https://www.findagrave.com.
110. "Ease Search for Hitchhiker In Murder," *Centralia Sentinel*, May 27, 1975.
111. Handwritten police notes (Harry L. Wright), CPD, May 10, 1975.
112. Police notes, May 10, 1975.
113. Police notes, May 10, 1975.
114. Police notes, May 10, 1975.
115. Police notes, May 10, 1975.
116. Police notes, May 10, 1975.
117. Handwritten police notes (David Hatley), CPD, undated.
118. "Man in Jail on '60 Charge," *Southern Illinoisan* (Carbondale, IL), December 13, 1965.
119. "To Report Obtaining Custody of Hi-Standard 22 Pistol," IBI investigative memorandum, June 3, 1975.
120. M.P. Fleisher, "Detectives Trap Suspects on Tape; Stolen Items Found," *Tampa Bay Times*, July 13, 1974.
121. *Sarasota Herald Tribune*, August 17, 1974.
122. "Circuit Court," *Centralia Evening Sentinel*, May 28, 1975.
123. Handwritten police notes, CPD, undated.
124. Police notes, undated.
125. "Obtaining Custody of Hi-Standard 22 Pistol."
126. "Obtaining Custody of Hi-Standard 22 Pistol."
127. Letter from Roger C. Thompson, criminalist, IBI, to Wayne A. Kersetetter, IBI, June 13, 1975.
128. "Circuit Court."
129. Police notes, undated.
130. "Circuit Court."
131. "David Wayne Hatley of Centralia," *Centralia Evening Sentinel*, July 10, 1975.
132. "Ease Search for Hitchhiker."
133. "David Hatley Criminal & Arrest Records," Radaris, https://radaris.com.

134. E-mail correspondence from Frost Hatley to author, July 24, 2024.
135. "Shots Fired in Chase-Arrest," *Daily Republican-Register* (Mount Carmel, IL), June 14, 1984.
136. "Frank Cipelle Obituary," A.J. Desmond & Sons, https://www.desmondfuneralhome.com.
137. "Father and Son Killed in Crash," *Detroit Free Press*, September 26, 1950.
138. "Frank Cipelle Obituary."
139. "To Report Information on Frank Cipelle," IBI investigative memorandum, July 14, 1975.
140. State of Illinois Department of Public Safety document, Bureau of Criminal Identification and Investigation, March 23, 1959.
141. Mathias v. Cipelle, United States Department of Justice / FBI memo to CPD, July 17, 1975.
142. "Clay to Testify on Stretcher Before Jury," *Champaign-Urbana (IL) Courier*, January 19, 1958.
143. "To report information on Frank Cipelle," State of Illinois Department of Law Enforcement Bureau of Identification, July 14, 1976.
144. "Clay to Testify on Stretcher."
145. Supplementary report, #75-325, June 13, 1976.
146. Memo from Simon Franklin, undated.
147. "Shakespeare Murder Anniversary."
148. Supplementary report, #75-325.
149. Supplementary report, #75-325.
150. Supplementary report, #75-325.
151. "To Report Information on Frank Cipelle," IBI investigative memorandum, October 26, 1976.
152. Urbana Police Department supplementary report, May 21, 1976.
153. Supplementary report, #75-325.
154. Cipelle, IBI investigative memorandum.
155. Cipelle, IBI investigative memorandum.
156. Porter, IBI interview.
157. "Sebring Future Bright After Newest Success," *Santa Cruz (CA) Sentinel*, March 24, 1975.
158. "Frank Cipelle Obituary."
159. Judith Joy, "40 Years After His Death, John Shakespeare's Murder Remains an Unsolved Mystery," *Centralia Sentinel*, December 6, 2015.
160. Interview with anonymous source, October 21, 2024.
161. "To Report the Interview with Bernard A. Gross," IBI investigative memorandum, November 16, 1976.

162. Porter, IBI interview.
163. Porter, IBI interview.
164. Gross, IBI interview.
165. Gross, IBI interview.
166. Gross, IBI interview.
167. Gross, IBI interview.
168. Gross, IBI interview.
169. Centralia, IL forum, topix.com, undated.
170. Handwritten police notes (CPD), September 21, 1976.
171. Gross, IBI interview.
172. "Voluntary Statement: Lee Hannon," CPD, undated.
173. "Voluntary Statement: Lee Hannon."
174. Porter, IBI interview.
175. Porter, IBI interview.
176. Porter, IBI interview.
177. Porter, IBI interview.
178. Letter from F.A. Paoletti, polygraph examiner, to Kermit Justice, CPD, November 18, 1976.
179. Joy, "40 Years After His Death."
180. Interview with David Agee conducted by Richard Sprehe, December 18, 2024.
181. Bernard "Bernie" Gross obituary, https://obituaries.morningsentinel.com.
182. "To Report a Telephonic Interview with Ron Goff," IBI investigative memorandum, October 18, 1976.
183. Goff, IBI interview.
184. Goff, IBI interview.
185. Handwritten police notes, CPD, September 9, 1976.
186. Goff, IBI interview.
187. Amber Grimes, "Teen Accuses Ex-Principal," *Belleville (IL) News-Democrat*, March 4, 1994.
188. "Tapes Will Be Allowed in Sex-Abuse Trial," *Belleville (IL) News-Democrat*, June 25, 1994.
189. "In Brief: Former Counselor Is Sentenced for Abuse," *Belleville (IL) News-Democrat*, November 11, 1995.
190. "Ronald Allen Goff," Adams Funeral Home, https://www.adamsfuneralhome.com.
191. "Voluntary Statement," CPD, unidentified subject, possibly John Schaler, undated.
192. Handwritten police notes, CPD, circa January 1976.
193. Goff, IBI interview.

194. Handwritten police notes, CPD, September 9, 1976.
195. "To Report Interview with [Redacted]," IBI investigative memorandum, October 12, 1976.
196. Porter, IBI interview.
197. [Redacted], IBI interview.
198. Handwritten police notes, CPD, circa January 1976.
199. [Redacted], IBI interview.
200. Handwritten police notes, CPD, May 19, 1975.
201. Handwritten police notes, CPD, circa January 1976.
202. Centralia, IL forum, topix.com.
203. "Detail Page," CPD, Marilyn A. Wilkinson, undated.
204. Handwritten police notes, Tony Cunningham, May 29, 1975.
205. Cunningham police notes.
206. "Night Riders or Vendettas," handwritten list of members, CPD files, undated.
207. Cunningham police notes.
208. Centralia, IL forum, topix.com.
209. Cunningham police notes.
210. Cunningham police notes.
211. Cunningham police notes.
212. "Voluntary Statement: Mark Miller," CPD, May 11, 1975.
213. "Voluntary Statement: Mark Miller."
214. "Voluntary Statement: Mark Miller."
215. "Voluntary Statement: Mark Miller."
216. "Voluntary Statement: Mark Miller."
217. "Voluntary Statement: Mark Miller."
218. "Voluntary Statement: Mark Miller."
219. "Voluntary Statement: Mark Miller."
220. "Detail Page," Marilyn A. Wilkinson.
221. Letter from H. Dwight Whitlock, polygraph examiner, IBI, to Simon Franklin, CPD, May 28, 1975.
222. Whitlock letter to Franklin, May 28, 1975.
223. Handwritten police notes, CPD, undated.
224. Letter from H. Dwight Whitlock, polygraph examiner, IBI, to Simon Franklin, CPD, June 10, 1975.
225. Handwritten police notes, CPD, undated.
226. "Detail Page," CPD, 1-9-885, Tony Cunningham, undated.
227. Handwritten police notes, CPD, undated.
228. Handwritten police notes, CPD, undated
229. "Five Charged in Robbery of Man," *Breese (IL) Journal*, March 4, 1976.

230. Tony Cunninham LinkedIn profile, https://www.linkedin.com.
231. "Centralia Man Faces Sexual Abuse Charges," WMIZ94.com, September 20, 2016, https://www.wmix94.com.
232. "Clinton County Circuit Court," *Breese (IL) Journal*, September 22, 2016.
233. "Two Inmates in Clinton County to Be Released from Illinois Department of Corrections During Week Ending March 19," *South Central Reporter*, March 11, 2022, https://southcentralreporter.com.
234. Interview with Vanessa Cunningham, August 16, 2024.
235. Cunningham, interview.
236. Cunningham, interview.
237. Supplementary report, Bill Flanigan, October 14, 1976.
238. Porter, IBI interview.
239. Porter, IBI interview.
240. Porter, IBI interview.
241. "To Report Information Received from Ruth Gant," CPD investigation report, December 2, 1976.
242. Handwritten police notes (conversation with Ralph Porter), CPD, undated.
243. "To Report Information received from William D. Flanigan," CPD investigation report, November 24, 1976.
244. Handwritten police notes, CPD, undated (circa October 1976).
245. "To Report Information Received from Don Vonderhiede," IBI investigative report, November 15, 1976.
246. Flanigan, CPD report.
247. "To Report Information Received from Charles T. Draffen," CPD investigation report, December 1, 1976.
248. Flanigan, CPD report.
249. Flanigan, CPD report.
250. Flanigan, CPD report.
251. Flanigan, CPD report.
252. Flanigan, CPD report.
253. "To Report Information from Harley Quillman, Pinckneyville, Ill.," CPD, December 3, 1976.
254. William Flanigan obituary, *Southern Illinoisan* (Carbondale, IL), April 5, 1987.
255. Letter from Sam Eller to John Shakespeare, undated, postmarked May 8, 1975.
256. "To Report Interview with Samuel L. Eller," IBI investigative memorandum, October 18, 1976.
257. Untitled police report, Samuel Lee Eller, September 16, 1975.
258. Eller, IBI interview, October 18, 1976.
259. Eller, police report, September 16, 1975.

260. "To Report Interview with Samuel Eller," IBI investigative memorandum, October 14, 1976.
261. Eller, IBI interview, October 14. 1976.
262. Second untitled police report, Samuel Lee Eller, undated.
263. Eller, police report, undated.
264. Eller, police report, undated.
265. Supplementary report, #75-325, October 10, 1976.
266. Supplementary report, #75-325.
267. Supplementary report, #75-325,
268. Handwritten police notes, CPD, October 14, 1976.
269. Katy Delay, *Gold and Freedom: A Biographical Sketch of Edward C. Harwood* (CreateSpace, 2013).
270. Delay, *Gold and Freedom.*
271. Letter from Albert F. Gibson to John Shakespeare, January 15, 1974.
272. "Statement of Administrator: Estate of John W. Shakespeare, Deceased," Internal Review Service, undated.
273. "In the Matter of the Estate of John W. Shakespeare, Deceased," petition accompanying administrator's final report, in the Circuit Court of Marion County, Illinois, June 19, 1980.
274. Los Angeles Police Bulletin, January 14, 1976.
275. Los Angeles Police Bulletin.
276. Letter from Roger C. Thompson, criminalist, IBI, to Robert Bullock, acting superintendent, IBI, October 27, 1976.
277. "Illinois Ex-Officials' Son Charged in Tractor Theft," *St. Louis Post-Dispatch*, August 5, 1962.
278. "To Report an Interview with Enos McGee," IBI investigative memorandum, April 4, 1977.
279. "To Report Interview with Sheriff Jerry Dall," IBI investigative memorandum, July 17, 1975.
280. "To Report Interview with David Moss, Moss Funeral Home," IBI investigative memorandum, July 16, 1975.
281. Moss, IBI interview.
282. "To Report Interview with Vernita Granda," IBI investigative memorandum, July 18, 1975.
283. Granda, IBI interview.
284. "To report an interview with Emil A. Garcia, President, Haag Hatchery, Inc.," IBI investigative memorandum, August 5, 1975.
285. "To Report Interview with Mrs. Dorothy Haag," IBI investigative memorandum, August 8, 1975.

286. McGee, IBI interview.
287. McGee, IBI interview.
288. "To Report Interview with Frank Crockett," IBI investigative memorandum, February 2, 1977.
289. Crockett, interview.
290. Crockett, interview.
291. Crockett, interview.
292. "Pair Captured in Tavern Robbery," *Belleville (IL) News-Democrat*, October 17, 1964.
293. "Battery Charge," *Mt. Vernon (IL) Register-News*, January 24, 1975.
294. "Indicted by Grand Jury Yesterday," *Mt. Vernon (IL) Register-News*, May 2, 1975.
295. "Court Report," *Mt. Vernon (IL) Register-News*, May 20, 1975.
296. "To Report Interview with Subject, Sgt. Lonnie Odle," CPD investigation report, November 11, 1976.
297. "Personal Identification: Randy Reyes," Granite City Police Department, July 1, 1975.
298. Handwritten police notes, author unknown, CPD, May 15, 1975.
299. "Breese Man Fined After Fight at Breese Products," *Breese (IL) Journal*, April 16, 1970.
300. "Grand Jury Indictments," *Centralia Sentinel*, May 27, 1975.
301. "Constitutional Rights and Warnings, Larry Luigs," May 29, 1975.
302. Illinois State Police Investigation Report, Roy Earl Schultz, September 19, 1975.
303. Stephen G. Freeman, "A Dime of Pure Gold," *Reader's Digest* (July 1972).
304. Freeman, "Dime of Pure Gold."
305. Freeman, "Dime of Pure Gold."
306. Freeman, "Dime of Pure Gold."
307. Freeman, "Dime of Pure Gold."
308. "Armed Coast Guard Arrest Three on Yacht," *Evening News* (Port Angeles, WA), August 10, 1971.
309. "Abandoned U.S. Crew Describes Yacht Hijacking," *Lawton (OK) Constitution*, August 16, 1971.
310. "Three on Trial for Attempted Piracy," *Redlands (CA) Daily Facts*, June 5, 1972.
311. "Third Suspect in Hijacking of Yacht Given Probation," *Independent* (Long Beach, CA), December 15, 1972.
312. Letter from John Wight, editor, *Centralia Sentinel*, to Mary Shakespeare, January 30, 1976.
313. Interview with John Wight, July 1, 2024.
314. Supplementary report, John A. Erickson, Sheriff's Office Madison County (Edwardsville, IL), March 26, 1975.

315. Erickson supplementary report.
316. Letter from Bill Weigel (Clayton, MO) to Centralia Police Department, June 3, 1975.
317. "To Report Information Obtained on Don Rhodes [*sic*]," IBI investigative memorandum, June 26, 1975.
318. Letter from Robert A. Walkington (Jerseyville, IL) to Kermit Justice, CPD, May 11, 1977.
319. Walkington letter to Justice.
320. Walkington letter to Justice.
321. Handwritten police notes, author unknown, CPD, June 15, 1975.
322. "Lucy Hanley in ref. to David Hanley," daily report record, CPD, May 13, 1975.
323. "Memo from Simon Franklin," (undated).
324. Interview with Mike Justice, August 23, 2024.
325. "John W. Shakespeare | Murdered May 8, 1975 | Centralia, Illinois," *Keep It Weird*, https://www.keepitweirdpodcast.com/shakespeare.

9. The Press, the City, and the Rumors

1. Articles about Shakespeare's murder appeared in newspapers all over the Midwest as well as in papers in Florida, Nebraska and Texas, among others.
2. John Wight, "Shakespeare Found Murdered," *Centralia Sentinel*, May 9, 1975.
3. Wight, "Shakespeare Found Murdered."
4. Wight, "Shakespeare Found Murdered."
5. Wight, "Shakespeare Found Murdered."
6. Wight, "Shakespeare Found Murdered."
7. Wight, "Shakespeare Found Murdered."
8. Wight, "Shakespeare Found Murdered."
9. Judith Joy, "40 Years After His Death, John Shakespeare's Murder Remains an Unsolved Mystery," *Centralia Sentinel*, December 6, 2015.
10. "Centralia Without a Police Chief," *Decatur (IL) Daily Review*, April 28, 1974.
11. "Obituary for Jack Sanders," Sutherland Funeral Homes, https://www.sutherlandfuneralhome.com.
12. C. Lentz, "An Evaluation of the Vincennes Trail Law Enforcement Major Case Squad" (thesis, Vincennes Trail Law Enforcement Commission, Salem, IL, 1978).
13. "HELP WANTED: The Vincennes Trail Law Enforcement Commission," *Effingham (IL) Daily News*, June 12, 1971.
14. "Obituary for Jack Sanders."

15. Copies of correspondence between both parties during this time are in the evidence files of the Centralia Police Department.
16. Letter from Kermit Justice, acting chief of police, CPD to Jack Sanders, Vincennes Trail Law Enforcement Commission, August 24, 1976.
17. Supplementary report #75-325, February 9, 1977.
18. "Police Chief Takes Leave of Absence," *The Times* (Streater, IL), June 19, 1976.
19. "Police Chief Takes Leave."
20. "Inquiry Ordered Into Centralia, Ill., Alleged Police Corruption," *St. Louis Post-Dispatch*, March 18, 1979.
21. "Inquiry Ordered Into Centralia."
22. "Inquiry Ordered Into Centralia."
23. "Inquiry Ordered Into Centralia."
24. Grand Jury card/list, June 25, 1979.
25. "No-Hold Barred Probe of Centralia PD Ordered," *Taylorville (IL) Daily Breeze Courier*, March 17, 1979.
26. "Centralia Police Cleared of Corruption Allegations," *Daily Republican-Register* (Mount Carmel, IL), July 9, 1982
27. "Centralia Police Cleared."
28. "Found Not Guilty," *Breese (IL) Journal*, April 28, 1977.
29. "Youth Killed in Robbery Attempt as Crowd Watches," *Herald and Review* (Decatur, IL), December 23, 1979.
30. "Brothers Slain by Centralia Police Buried After Private Funeral Services," *Southern Illinoisan* (Carbondale, IL), December 24, 1979.
31. "Youth Killed in Robbery."
32. "Conspiracy Charges Filed in Armed Robbery," *Evansville (IN) Courier and Press*, December 29, 1979.
33. The Devil's Playground | Missing Persons Awareness, missinginillinois.org.
34. "Centralia Police Chief Resigns Amid Investigation of City Councilman Case," X95radio.com, September 6, 2016.
35. Interview with Doug Krutsinger, June 27, 2024.
36. "Supplemental Report," Chula Vista (CA) Police Department, Mary Alice Gaddy, September 24, 1982.
37. Letter from L.R. Huffman to "Police Department," April 29, 2002.
38. Huffman, letter.
39. Letter from Angelo G. MacDonald, Office of the District Attorney, Bronx County, to Chris Belling, Assistant District Attorney, Eric County (NY), December 24, 1997; letter from Richard B. Schaeffer, District Attorney, Queens County, July 16, 1996; and Anne Gutman, Assistant District Attorney, Kings County (NY), August 1, 1997.

ABOUT THE AUTHORS

Cary O'Dell is a native of Illinois and a graduate of Southern Illinois University in Carbondale. He now lives in Virginia and works for the Library of Congress. He is the author of several books, including *Johnny Bob: The Life and Times of Johnny Bob Harrell*, *Bucky's Dome*, and *Virginia Marmaduke: A Journey in Print from Carbondale to Chicago*.

Richard L. Sprehe is a retired pharmacist now residing in Town and Country, Missouri. He holds degrees from SIU-Carbondale and the St. Louis College of Pharmacy. At the time of John Shakespeare's murder, Richard was employed by Byrd-Watson Drug and Campbell Ambulance Service in Centralia, Illinois. Richard and his wife, Varasteh, have two daughters and one grandson.

0. Letter from Detective Steve Prather, CPD, to L.R. Huffman, May 3, 2002.
1 At least fifteen letters were exchanged between L.R. Huffman and Detective Prather, from April 29, 2002, until April 20, 2003.
42. Huffman-Prather letters.
43. Huffman-Prather letters.
44. Sean Gardiner, "The Con Man," *Newsday*, December 7, 2003.
45. Krutsinger, interview.
46. Krutsinger, interview.
47. Krutsinger, interview.
48. In one newspaper article (unknown source and unknown date), there is one fleeting mention, made by former CPD Chief Arland Speidel, of a police auction of "surplus," but he does not confirm that any Shakespeare evidence was among those items.
49. Handwritten police notes (William Flanigan), CPD, October 13, 1976.
50. Ashley Casseday and Stephen Garland, hosts, *Keep It Weird*, podcast, "Murder in the Midwest," 2018, https://www.keepitweirdpodcast.com.